£10.08

# katie
## stewart's
### GOOD FOOD

# katie
## stewart's
## GOOD FOOD

RECIPE PHOTOGRAPHS BY PHILIP WEBB

TED SMART

NOTE

1. Standard level spoon measurements are used in all recipes.
1 tablespoon = one 15 ml spoon
1 teaspoon = one 5 ml spoon

2. Both imperial and metric measurements have been given in all recipes. Use one set
of measurements only and not a mixture of both.

3. Eggs should be medium (size 3) unless otherwise stated.

4. Ovens should be preheated to the specific temperature – if using a fan assisted
oven, follow manufacturer's instructions for adjusting the time and the temperature.

PUBLISHING DIRECTOR: Laura Bamford
SENIOR EDITOR: Sasha Judelson
EDITORIAL ASSISTANT: Katey Day
ART DIRECTOR: Keith Martin
SENIOR DESIGNER: Louise Leffler
DESIGNER: Ginny Zeal
PRODUCTION CONTROLLER: Melanie Frantz
INDEXER: Hilary Bird
PHOTOGRAPHER: Philip Webb/Woman's Journal/Robert Harding Syndication

First published in Great Britain in 1997 by Hamlyn
an imprint of Reed Consumer Books Limited
Michelin House, 81 Fulham Road, London SW3 6RB
and Auckland, Melbourne, Singapore and Toronto

This edition published in 1997 for The Book People,
Hall Wood Avenue, Haydock, St Helens WA11 9UL
by Hamlyn

Text copyright © 1997 Katie Stewart
Design copyright © 1997 Reed International Books Limited
Illustrations copyright © IPC Magazines, Robert Harding Syndication
ISBN 1-85613-316-8

A CIP catalogue record for this book is available from the British Library.

Produced by Mandarin Offset
Printed in Hong Kong

# Contents

# Introduction

Cooking has been an all consuming passion of mine for a long time now. I could never have asked for anything more satisfying than to have a career in a subject that would otherwise have become a hobby. I have been the Food Editor for *Woman's Journal* magazine  since the 1960s. I was trained in the traditional school, but in the years that have passed the style of cooking has changed and become more international, ingredients have become more diverse and food fashions have come and gone. It's been hard work keeping up with it all, but thoroughly enjoyable hard work.

I have always considered myself a kind of 'middle man', with the task of finding out the latest, up-to-date information, sussing out the best recipes and passing them on – like friends who swap recipes. I write about the things that interest me and produce recipes I like to cook, there is no other way. You have to be genuinely enthusiastic about your own ideas and hope that your readers will like them too. By being meticulous and thorough I have built up a reputation for being accurate, for producing recipes that work and I'm proud of that. I cook in my home kitchen in Sussex and test taste my recipes on willing friends.

This is a collection of recipes published in *Woman's Journal* over the last few years. They are recent because the style of cooking changes so quickly that to have gone any further back could have made the recipes seem a little dated. I like recipes that are relatively easy, although I'm not averse to spending hours in the kitchen for something special. I feel strongly about working within the seasons – to take the best ingredients and keep the recipes simple seems like the right way to me. This is not a cookbook that covers the basics, nor is it one for any particular occasion. This is a very carefully chosen collection of recipes  that I like, as diverse as I can make them. Alongside are the stunning colour photographs just as they appeared on the magazine pages. Recipe writing is a skill that shouldn't be underestimated. A recipe has to contain all the necessary

information, be unambiguous and easy to follow from start to finish. I write my recipes in stages, so if you take your eye off the recipe while working you can get back to where you were again without having to start at the beginning and read right through. There are preparation and cooking times, so at a glance you can see if it's a long or a short method and there are special tips to guide you through the tricky bits. As is necessary in a cookery book, recipes are grouped into sections but this doesn't mean that a starter wouldn't make a light lunch or a pasta recipe a good supper. Please feel free to use them as you wish. The recipes are suitable for family consumption or for parties. I don't really believe in special recipes for entertaining; for friends you cook the food you like best and the recipes you are good at.

On a magazine the trick is team work. I certainly don't produce all this beautiful material myself. For 6 years Caroline Young worked alongside me, developing ideas which, at times, have been nothing short of brilliant. Many of her recipes are included. The recipe photographs which appear regularly in *Woman's Journal* and are reproduced here are mouthwatering to look at. I am allowed to work with the very best food photographers and none is better than Phillip Webb whose work this is. Every month I take my ingredients and cook in his studio kitchen for the next magazine issue. After this the cookery pages are laid out by the hungry art department and finally the work is read through by eagle-eyed sub-editors who fit the lines and make sure there are no missing ingredients or mistakes. I thank them all for their input.

My recipes are like old friends because I cook them regularly for my own family, often updating them and making little changes here and there. It's always a good idea to follow a recipe as it's written the first time, after that you can add your own touches and hopefully slot many of 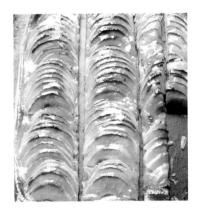 these into your own repertoire of tried and tested recipes.

*Happy Cooking!*

*Katie Stewart*

# Soups and Snacks

There is always a day when time is short, that's when you need a good snack recipe. Snacks are essentially very simple – a baked potato with a topping or a home-made spread with toast. Soups with chunky pieces of vegetable, beans or pasta make excellent snack lunches, and can be made ahead and heated just before serving. Add hot breads or a simple green salad.

*Pear and Blue Cheese Crostini*

# Pear and Blue Cheese Crostini

4 slices white bread
2–3 tablespoons olive oil
2 fresh ripe pears
100 g (4 oz) blue cheeses –
    Roquefort, Dolcelatte or
    Stilton

**Serves 2–4**
Preparation time: 10 minutes
Cooking time: 5 minutes

**1** Heat the grill to hot and set the grill rack about 7.5 cm (3 inches) from the heat source. Arrange the bread slices on a baking tray and brush with olive oil. Slide under the grill to brown. Turn the bread slices, brush with olive oil once again and then grill the other side until golden brown.

**2** Meanwhile, peel, core and slice the pears lengthways. Arrange slices of pear on each toasted bread slice.

**3** Cover the pears with slices of which ever blue cheese you have chosen. Return to the heat and grill until the cheese is bubbling. Serve at once.

# Smoked Mackerel Mousse

225 g (8 oz) smoked mackerel
    – about 2 medium fillets
50 g (2 oz) butter
100 g (4 oz) cream cheese
juice ½ lemon
2 teaspoons horseradish relish
salt and freshly milled pepper
4 tablespoons single cream

**Serves 4–6**
Preparation time: 15 minutes

**1** Pull away the skin from each smoked mackerel fillet and flake the flesh onto a plate.

**2** In a mixing bowl cream the butter (at room temperature) until soft, then beat in the cream cheese. Add the flaked smoked mackerel, lemon juice, horseradish relish, a seasoning of salt and freshly milled pepper and the cream and beat to a smooth mixture. Or, place all ingredients in a food processor and blend to a smooth purée. Serve as a starter with hot French bread or dry toast slices.

# Crisp Pastry Layers with Mixed Mushrooms and Cream

**1** On a floured work surface, roll the pastry to a square of about 17.5 cm (7 inches) and a depth of no less than 5 mm (¼ inch). Trim the edges and cut the pastry piece in half lengthways and across to make 4 smaller squares. Slide the pastry onto a baking tray and chill for 20 minutes.

**2** Heat the oven to 200°C (400°F or gas no. 6). With the point of a small knife, score the surface of each pastry square in a criss-cross pattern. Brush with beaten egg and sprinkle with sesame seeds. Set in the oven to bake for 15 minutes, until well risen and golden.

**3** Meanwhile prepare the filling. Slice the chestnut mushrooms thickly and leave the oyster mushrooms whole. Melt the garlic and herb butter in a frying pan, add the mushrooms and cook gently for a few minutes to soften. Allow some of the mushroom juices to evaporate, then gently stir in the crème fraîche and bring the mixture to a simmer. Season to taste.

**4** Split the baked puff pastry shapes with a knife – they will come apart quite easily. Set the base of each one on a warm serving plate. Spoon over the mixed mushrooms and sauce. Cover with the pretty pastry tops and serve.

250 g (9 oz) ready-made puff
   pastry
beaten egg to glaze
sesame seeds for sprinkling
450 g (1 lb) mixed
   mushrooms – chestnut and
   oyster
50 g (2 oz) prepared garlic
   and herb butter
2 tablespoons crème fraîche
salt and freshly milled pepper

**Serves 4**
Preparation time: 40 minutes
Cooking time: 15 minutes

# Garlic Cheese and Sweet Pepper Tarts

**1** On a floured work surface, roll the puff pastry to an oblong of about 22.5 x 30 cm (9 x 12 inches). Trim the pastry edges (see Katie's Tip) then cut the whole pastry lengthways and across to make 4 oblong pieces – the pieces will finish up being about 10 x 15 cm (4 x 6 inches). Arrange the puff pastry pieces on a baking tray – they should all fit neatly together without touching. Chill for 20 minutes while preparing the filling.

**2** Quarter the peppers lengthways and remove the seeds. Crowd the pepper pieces on a baking tray (skin sides uppermost) and brush with olive oil. Place under a hot grill to char the skins. Cut the peppers into chunky pieces.

**3** Slice the aubergines and arrange slices on a baking tray. Brush slices with olive oil and set under the grill until browned, turn once to brown both sides.

**4** Heat the oven to 200°C (400°F or gas no. 6). Spread a quarter of the garlic and herb cheese in the centre of each puff pastry piece. Set an arrangement of sweet pepper pieces, aubergine and salami slices over the cheese base.

**5** Turn in the edges of each pastry oblong, pinching the corners to make small 'box' shapes. Brush the pastry edges with beaten egg. Set filled tarts in the heated oven and bake for 15–20 minutes. Serve hot.

250 g (9 oz) ready-made puff pastry
2 sweet peppers – red and yellow
4–6 tablespoons olive oil
1 large aubergine
50 g (2 oz) garlic and herb soft cheese
50 g (2 oz) thinly sliced salami, about 8 slices
beaten egg to glaze

**Serves 4**
Preparation time: 40 minutes
Cooking time: 15–20 minutes

---

### Katie's Tip

Puff pastry is made by folding together layers of fat and dough. After rolling out puff pastry you must free the pastry layers by cutting all the pastry edges with a knife. Then the layers will rise beautifully in the heat of the oven. Use a sharp kitchen knife and dip the blade in flour to make sure you get clean cuts.

# Smoked Haddock Pâté

450 g (1 lb) smoked haddock
 fillet
100 g (4 oz) butter
225 g (8 oz) curd cheese
freshly milled pepper
1 tablespoon lemon juice
lemon slices and bay leaf to
 garnish

**Serves 4–6**
Preparation time: 15 minutes
Cooking time: 5 minutes

**1** Cut the smoked haddock into 4 pieces. Melt half the butter in a 25 cm (10 inch) frying pan (with a lid) and add the haddock pieces. Cover with the pan lid and cook gently over the heat until the fish is tender – about 5 minutes. Allow to cool.

**2** Carefully lift away the fish skin. Turn the haddock flesh and all the buttery juices from the pan into the bowl of a food processor. Add the curd cheese, a seasoning of freshly milled pepper and the lemon juice and blend to a purée.

**3** Turn the mixture into a serving dish and spread level, mounding it slightly in the centre. Melt the remaining butter and spoon over. Place two slices of lemon and a bay leaf on top for garnish and chill.

# Egg and Smoked Salmon-Filled Hot Rolls

2 ciabatta rolls
1 tablespoon olive oil
2 slices smoked salmon
2 eggs
freshly milled black pepper
4 tinned artichoke hearts or
 sliced artichoke hearts in
 olive oil from a jar
2 tablespoons oil and vinegar
 dressing
1 teaspoon grainy mustard

**Serves 2**
Preparation time: 20 minutes
Cooking time: 20 minutes

**1** Cut the top third from each roll horizontally, then scoop out the soft crumbs. Brush the inside of each roll with olive oil, line with a folded slice of smoked salmon, then crack in an egg. Season the egg with freshly milled black pepper.

**2** Heat the oven to 180°C (350°F or gas no. 4). Set a large square of foil on a baking tray and arrange filled rolls inside. Draw the sides of the foil over the top of the rolls to make a baggy parcel. Bake in the heated oven for 20 minutes, then open the foil and return to the oven for a further few minutes, until eggs are cooked and rolls are crisp.

**3** Meanwhile slice the artichoke hearts in half and turn them in the dressing with the grainy mustard. Set rolls on each serving plate, add artichoke hearts and dressing and serve.

# Smoked Haddock and Sweetcorn Chowder

*Poach smoked haddock to make a stock, then use the stock to flavour the soup – simple!*

**1** Cut the smoked haddock into about 4 pieces. Put in a medium saucepan with 600 ml (1 pint) water, the bay leaf, parsley stalks and the slice of lemon. Bring to a simmer, cover and cook for 5–6 minutes. With a slotted spoon lift out the fish pieces and, when cool enough to handle, remove the skin and flake the fish. Strain and reserve the fish stock. Peel and finely chop the onion and then peel and dice the potatoes.

**2** Heat the butter in a large saucepan. Add the chopped onion and sauté gently to soften but not brown – about 5 minutes. Add the diced potato and reserved fish stock. Bring to the boil, then cover and simmer for about 15 minutes or until the potato pieces are just tender. Stir in the milk and the sweetcorn. Stir until the soup is just simmering. Draw off the heat, add the pieces of smoked haddock, check the seasoning and add lemon juice to taste. Stir in 2 or 3 tablespoons of cream just before serving.

450 g (1 lb) smoked haddock
   fillet
1 bay leaf
few parsley stalks
slice lemon
1 large onion
450 g (1 lb) maincrop
   potatoes
25 g (1 oz) butter
600 ml (1 pint) milk
1 x 425 g tin creamed-style
   sweetcorn
salt and freshly milled pepper
juice ½ lemon
2–3 tablespoons single cream

**Serves 4**
Preparation time: 15 minutes
Cooking time: 25–30 minutes

---

### Katie's Tip

When any soup recipe includes milk it's usually added at a later stage. Always reheat the soup gently just to serving temperature – boiling will spoil the texture and the flavour.

---

# Smoked Mackerel Platter with Baked Shallots

250 g (9 oz) shallots
2 tablespoons olive oil
3–4 smoked mackerel fillets
freshly milled pepper

**Serves 4**
Preparation time: 10 minutes
Cooking time: 40–45 minutes

**1** Heat the oven to 190°C (375°F or gas no. 5). Leave the shallots unpeeled (when cooked, they will have a soft texture, so they can easily be pressed from their skins) and turn them in the olive oil. Put the shallots into a casserole, cover and set in the heated oven. Bake for 40–45 minutes or until knife-tip tender.

**2** Arrange the mackerel fillets on a platter and add the hot shallots. To extend the platter further, you could add slices of toast spread with Smoked Mackerel Mousse (see page 10).

**3** Dust the platter with pepper. Serve with a green salad and hot accompaniments, such as new potatoes or hot crusty bread.

# Mixed Vegetable Soup with Cheese

*Just as satisfying as any fish or meat soup, this cheese and vegetable mixture is delicately flavoured and filling.*

1 green sweet pepper
4 medium carrots
4 stalks celery
100 g (4 oz) Lancashire cheese
65 g (2½ oz) butter
600 ml (1 pint) vegetable
  stock
2 tablespoons plain flour
300 ml (½ pint) milk
salt and freshly milled pepper
grated nutmeg

**Serves 4**
Preparation time: 25 minutes
Cooking time: 30 minutes

**1** Halve and deseed the green pepper, then slice lengthways and across, and chop finely. Pare and finely chop the carrots. Rinse the celery, snap the stalks and pull away the strings, then slice the stalks lengthways and across into small dice. Coarsely grate the cheese.

**2** Melt 25 g (1 oz) of butter in a large saucepan, add the vegetables and stew gently for 5 minutes, covered with the pan lid.
Add the stock and bring to the boil. Lower the heat, re-cover and simmer gently for 15 minutes.

**3** Meanwhile, in a second smaller saucepan, melt the remaining butter. Stir in the flour and cook for 1–2 minutes, then gradually stir in the milk, beating well all the time to make a smooth white sauce. Season with salt, pepper and a grating of nutmeg. Let the sauce simmer gently for about 5 minutes, then draw the pan off the heat, add the grated cheese and stir until the cheese has melted.

**4** Stir the cheese sauce into the pan of vegetables and stock and mix to make a creamy soup. Reheat the soup for a moment or two (but don't let the contents boil), ladle into hot soup bowls and then serve.

# White Bean and Pasta Soup with Sun-Dried Tomatoes

*Stew these flavouring vegetables gently and for some time to extract their juices.*

2 medium onions

2 large carrots

1 head fennel

4 cloves garlic

3 tablespoons olive oil

1 teaspoon caster sugar

1 litre (1¾ pints) vegetable
  stock

25 g (1 oz) small soup pasta

1 x 432 g tin cannellini beans

6 sun-dried tomatoes in oil

salt and freshly milled pepper

2 tablespoons chopped fresh
  parsley

50–75 g (2–3 oz) grated
  Parmesan cheese to serve

**Serves 4–6**

Preparation time: 20 minutes

Cooking time: 30 minutes

**1** Peel and finely chop the onions. Pare and dice the carrots. Trim the fennel and shred across the head to slice finely. Peel the garlic and crush or finely chop.

**2** Heat the oil in a large saucepan. Add the prepared onion, carrot and fennel. Sprinkle with the sugar. Cover with the pan lid and stew gently for 20 minutes to soften them. Stir in the garlic. Add the vegetable stock and bring to a simmer.

**3** Stir in the soup pasta and cook for 6–8 minutes or until the pasta is tender. Meanwhile, drain and rinse the cannellini beans. Fork the sun-dried tomatoes from their jar and chop them finely. Stir the beans and chopped tomatoes into the soup and heat gently, then check the seasoning and stir in the parsley. Serve in bowls topped with a good sprinkling of grated Parmesan.

---

## Katie's Tip

For a good soup flavour I always fry the flavouring vegetables gently at an early stage. It draws the juices and, if the vegetables brown a little, it also adds flavour and colour to the soup. Never use anything less than butter or olive oil for frying, because the taste is so important.

# Winter Cabbage, Bacon and Ravioli Soup

**1** Trim the bacon rashers and cut into 1 cm (½ inch) pieces. Peel and finely chop the onion. Peel and crush the garlic. Shred the cabbage very finely across the leaves. Cut the carrot into thin diagonal slices.
**2** Put the bacon in a saucepan with the olive oil and cook over a moderate heat to draw the bacon dripping. Add the chopped onion to the pan and cook, stirring occasionally, until the onion and bacon are beginning to brown. Stir in the crushed garlic.
**3** Add the chicken stock and bring to the boil. Add the carrots and simmer for 5 minutes. Add the shredded cabbage and the ravioli to the pan. Bring back to a simmer and cook gently, uncovered, until the ravioli are just tender – about 4–5 minutes. Stir in the chopped parsley. Ladle into hot soup bowls, sprinkle with grated Parmesan and serve.

5 streaky bacon rashers
1 medium onion
2 cloves garlic
¼ green cabbage
1 large carrot
1 tablespoon olive oil
1.4 litres (2½ pints) chicken stock
225 g (8 oz) fresh ravioli – preferably cheese filled
2 tablespoons chopped fresh parsley
grated Parmesan cheese to serve

**Serves 4**
Preparation time: 15 minutes
Cooking time: 25 minutes

---

## BIG DIPPER

- Drain 1 x 440 g tin chickpeas, rinse under cold water and put in a food processor bowl.
- Peel and crush 2 cloves of garlic and add along with a good seasoning of salt and freshly milled pepper.
- Add 2 tablespoons tahini (sesame paste), 2 tablespoons olive oil and 2–3 tablespoons squeezed lemon juice. Cover and blend to a purée.
- Turn the mixture into a serving bowl. Drizzle with a little extra olive oil and sprinkle with paprika.
Serve with hot pitta bread or warmed wholemeal rolls. Add a green salad and sliced ripe tomatoes for a quick and easy lunch. Serves 3–4.

# Split Baked Potatoes with Onions in Soured Cream, Egg and Green Olives

2 baking potatoes
olive oil for brushing
2 eggs
1 large onion
1 x 142 ml carton soured
  cream
salt and freshly milled black
  pepper
6–8 pitted green olives

**Serves 2**
Preparation time: 20 minutes
Cooking time: 1 hour

**1** Heat the oven to 220°C (425°F or gas no. 7). Scrub and dry the potatoes, then rub with olive oil. Prick each one in a couple of places, set in the heated oven and bake for 45 minutes to 1 hour until soft. Add the eggs to a pan of boiling salted water, simmer for 8 minutes to cook, then drain.

**2** Peel the onion leaving it whole, cut into slices and separate out the rings. Place these in a bowl, cover with boiling water and let them stand for about 10 minutes – this draws the strong flavour and tenderises the onion a little. Drain the onion rings and chill them. Then combine with the soured cream and a seasoning of salt and black pepper. Keep chilled until serving time.

**3** Slice the potatoes open in quarters and set on individual serving plates. Pile the chilled onions on top – the combination of hot and cold is delicious. Shell and halve the eggs, adding them and a few green olives to each plate.

---

### Katie's Tip
Hard-boiled eggs can flake or break when you cut them, but not if you dip the blade of the knife you are using in cold water first. Then eggs will halve or quarter cleanly and look much more attractive.

# Fresh Spinach and Nutmeg Soup

**1** Rinse spinach in cold water and tear away the stem and midribs. Peel and finely chop the onion and peel and crush the garlic.

**2** Melt 40 g (1½ oz) of the butter in a medium saucepan and stir in the flour. Cook gently for a few minutes. Gradually add the milk, stirring well, and bring to the boil to make a thin white sauce. Season with salt and freshly milled pepper. Simmer for 2–3 minutes, then draw off the heat.

**3** Meanwhile melt the remaining butter in a large saucepan. Add the chopped onion and cook gently for about 5 minutes to soften the onion. Stir in the garlic. Add the washed spinach leaves (with no extra liquid), cover the pan and allow spinach leaves to wilt.

**4** Add the seasoned white sauce and stir to mix. Turn the soup mixture into a food processor bowl or blender and buzz to a purée – the colour will be bright green. Return to the soup pan.

**5** Stir in the stock, check the seasoning and add plenty of freshly grated nutmeg – taste to get the flavour you like. Reheat the soup for serving and swirl in the cream off the heat.

450 g (1 lb) fresh leaf spinach
1 medium onion
1 clove garlic
75 g (3 oz) butter
25 g (1 oz) flour
600 ml (1 pint) milk
salt and freshly milled pepper
300 ml (½ pint) vegetable
  stock
grated nutmeg
4 tablespoons single cream

**Serves 4–6**
Preparation time: 20 minutes
Cooking time: 15 minutes

---

### DINNER JACKETS

The humble baked potato can be elevated to great heights with a clever topping. Here are a few of my favourite fillings:

• Seasoned soured cream and chopped smoked salmon

• Hot ratatouille with grated Parmesan cheese

• A soft cheese such as Boursin with herbs or pepper

• A spicy tomato and avocado salsa

• Sliced onions cooked in olive oil until golden and crisp bacon bits

• Sliced mushrooms fried in garlic butter

• Spoonfuls of pesto sauce with a soft, mild-flavoured goat's cheese (pictured)

# Falafel with Yoghurt and Mint Dip

**1** Drain the chickpeas, rinse them well and drain again. Peel and finely chop the onion and peel and mash the garlic.

**2** Put the chickpeas in a mixing bowl and mash with a fork until they form a smooth, even consistency. Add the finely chopped onion and the garlic and mix. Add the coriander, cumin, chilli, a good seasoning of salt and pepper, the chopped parsley and egg and mix thoroughly.

**3** Take spoonfuls of the mixture and shape into balls with floured fingers, then roll lightly in flour to coat and press each one to flatten slightly – you should get about 12 falafels.

**4** Heat about 2.5 cm (1 inch) of oil in a frying pan and shallow fry about 4–6 falafels at a time, first one side then the other until hot and lightly browned. Drain on absorbent kitchen paper and serve hot with Yoghurt and Mint Dip. These are delicious served as a snack with a green salad and hot pitta bread.

**Yoghurt and Mint Dip:** Combine 200 ml (7 fl oz) thick Greek-style yoghurt with a seasoning of salt and freshly milled pepper and 2 tablespoons chopped fresh mint. Mix well.

2 x 440 g tins chickpeas
1 medium onion
2 cloves garlic
2 teaspoons ground coriander
1 teaspoon ground cumin
½ teaspoon chilli powder
salt and freshly milled pepper
2 tablespoons chopped fresh
  parsley
1 egg
flour for coating
olive oil for shallow frying
Yoghurt and Mint Dip to
  serve (recipe below)

**Serves 4**
Preparation time: 20 minutes
Cooking time: 10 minutes

---

### Katie's Tip

Tinned beans and chickpeas come in useful in lots of ways. They are already cooked and only require a quick rinse in cold water before using. Add them to a vegetable ragoût or chilli. Or, even better, use them in salads when you can mix two or more colours. For the best flavour, rinse tinned beans or chickpeas, cover with cold water and bring to the boil, then drain. Add your favourite oil and vinegar dressing while they are still hot – they will soak up the flavour and the salad will taste even better.

# Starters and Party Nibbles

Anything can make a starter, if
served in a small enough portion.
For special occasions there are a
variety of starters and eye-
catching party nibbles here – some
simple, some more sophisticated,
but none that are complicated.
Hot starters are a pleasant surprise
for guests, prepare ahead then you
can make short work of the
finishing-off stage.

*Salad of Green Beans with
Butter Beans in a Lemon Dressing*

# Salad of Green Beans with Butter Beans in a Lemon Dressing

225 g (8 oz) French beans

1 x 220 g tin butter beans

salt and freshly milled pepper

1 lemon

6 tablespoons extra virgin
  olive oil

2 tablespoons chopped fresh
  parsley

**Serves 3**

Preparation time: 5 minutes

Cooking time: 5–6 minutes

**1** Trim the green beans, add to boiling salted water and cook for 5–6 minutes until just tender, then drain. Turn the beans into a mixing bowl. Drain the butter beans in a colander and rinse under cold water. Pick out any loose skins and discard them. Add the butter beans to the warm green beans.

**2** Add a seasoning of salt and freshly milled pepper. Grate in a little lemon rind – about ¼ of the lemon – then add the squeezed juice from the whole lemon. Finally add the extra virgin olive oil. Toss the bean salad and taste for seasoning.

**3** Spoon the beans onto 3 individual serving plates. Spoon over any dressing, dividing it equally. Give a final seasoning of freshly milled pepper and sprinkle with chopped parsley. Serve with slices of wholemeal bread.

---

### MEGA BITES

I try to make party nibbles interesting, flavoursome and preferably bite-sized. Here are some of my successes:

• Wafer-thin slices of best Italian Milano salami

• Fresh take-away sushi rolls with soy sauce for dipping

• Hot crostini with a Mediterranean tapenade topping

• Herb marinated olives

• Smoked fish canapés – mini melba toasts topped with a choice of smoked salmon, smoked eel or taramasalata

• Home-made tarragon mayonnaise with cucumber sticks for dipping

• Hollowed-out cherry tomatoes filled with seasoned cream cheese and topped with lumpfish caviar (pictured) or chopped smoked salmon

# Steamed Vegetables in a Marinade served with Walnut Bread

**1** Prepare the vegetables according to kind. Peel, then cut the carrots lengthways and across into short sticks. Separate the cauliflower head into small florets. Trim the courgettes – do not peel, simply pare strips from the green skin for effect – and cut courgettes into chunks, everything should be approximately bite-sized pieces.

**2** Measure the vinegar for the marinade into a large mixing bowl. Add the soft brown sugar, herbs and a seasoning of salt and freshly milled pepper. Peel and crush the garlic and add to the marinade along with the bay leaves.

**3** Steam the vegetables in batches for 4–8 minutes, until tender crisp. Add the hot vegetables to the marinade as they are cooked. Add the apricots and the black olives – rinsed if the olives are in brine. Add the olive oil. Cool mixture to room temperature. Marinate for 24 hours. Turn into a serving bowl. Let guests spoon vegetables and some of the marinade onto individual serving plates. Serve with thick slices of walnut or wholemeal bread to mop up the delicious juices.

2 medium carrots
1 small head cauliflower
3 courgettes
100 g (4 oz) ready-to-eat
   dried apricots
25–75 g (1–3 oz) pitted black
   olives
walnut or wholemeal bread
   to serve

FOR THE MARINADE:

75 ml (3 fl oz) red wine
   vinegar or cider vinegar
2 tablespoons soft brown
   sugar
1 teaspoon herbes de
   Provence
salt and freshly milled pepper
1–2 cloves garlic
2 bay leaves
175 ml (6 fl oz) olive oil

**Serves 6**
Preparation time: 20 minutes,
   plus marinating time
Cooking time: 20–25 minutes

# Peppered Cheese and Fruit

**1** Turn the curd cheese into a bowl and, with a fork, mix in a good seasoning of salt and freshly milled pepper. Divide into 4 portions and spoon onto a plate. Sprinkle with pinches of cracked pepper (also called steak pepper) and chill until serving time.
**2** Separate out the radicchio leaves and select 4–6 of the best cup-shaped ones (you can put more than one together). Spoon the cheese into each cup and arrange on a serving platter. Slice the figs lengthways in quarters and tuck around the cheese. (You could use sliced strawberries and cucumber or peaches and blueberries as an alternative.) Spoon Lemon and Honey Dressing over, sprinkle with toasted pine kernels and serve with slices of toasted French bread.

**Lemon and Honey Dressing:** Mix 2 tablespoons each of lemon juice, clear honey and olive oil. Season with salt and pepper.

225 g (8 oz) curd cheese
salt and freshly milled pepper
cracked pepper for sprinkling
1 small head radicchio
4 fresh figs
Lemon and Honey Dressing
   (recipe below)
1 tablespoon toasted pine
   kernels
toasted French bread to serve

**Serves 4**
Preparation time: 15 minutes,
   plus chilling time

# Onion and Goat's Cheese Tart

*Slices of tangy goat's cheese perfectly balance the flavour of a cheese pastry base with a sweet onion topping.*

**1** Sift the flour and baking powder into a medium mixing bowl. Add the butter, cut in pieces, and rub in with your fingertips. Stir in the grated Parmesan. Measure the milk and set aside with the dry ingredients for the pastry.
**2** Peel the onions, then slice thinly and separate out the rings. Heat the oil in a frying pan (with a lid) or a large saucepan. Add the onions, sprinkle with the sugar and cover with the pan lid. Cook the onions gently for 20 minutes, stirring occasionally – they should be soft but not browned. Cut the goat's cheese into 5 thick slices.
**3** Heat the oven to 190°C (375°F or gas no. 5). Add the milk to the pastry ingredients and mix to a soft dough. Turn onto a floured work surface and roll into a circle about 20–22.5 cm (8–9 inches) in diameter. Prick the pastry with the floured prongs of a fork and slide onto a baking tray. Arrange the slices of goat's cheese over the pastry, then fork the cooked onions over the top. Set in the preheated oven, bake for 20 minutes. Cut in slices and serve warm.

225 g (8 oz) self-raising flour
1 teaspoon baking powder
25 g (1 oz) butter
25 g (1 oz) grated Parmesan
   cheese
150 ml (¼ pint) milk
450 g (1 lb) onions
2 tablespoons olive oil
1 tablespoon caster sugar
1 x 100 g (4 oz) log-shaped
   goat's cheese

**Serves 4–6**
Preparation time: 40 minutes
Cooking time: 20 minutes

# Hot Spinach and Cheese Gratin

*A layer of creamed spinach with a cheese soufflé topping.*

900 g (2 lb) leaf spinach
300 ml (½ pint) milk
1 slice onion
1 bay leaf
40 g (1½ oz) butter
25 g (1 oz) plain flour
salt and freshly milled pepper
grated nutmeg
50 g (2 oz) grated Parmesan
　cheese
2 eggs

**Serves 6**

Preparation time: 40 minutes
Cooking time: 35–40 minutes

**1** Pull away centre ribs and rinse spinach in cold water. Lift the spinach directly into a large saucepan, add no water – there will be sufficient clinging to the leaves. Cover with the pan lid and cook over a moderate heat for 3–4 minutes or until the spinach has wilted. Turn the spinach into a colander and press with a potato masher to drain thoroughly. Place spinach leaves in a food processor and buzz to chop finely.

**2** Meanwhile, infuse the milk with the onion slice and bay leaf for 5–6 minutes, then strain the warm milk into a jug. Melt the butter in the rinsed, hot pan. Stir in the flour and cook gently for 1 minute. Gradually stir in the infused milk, beating well all the time to get a smooth sauce. Bring to a simmer, season with salt and freshly milled pepper and a grating of nutmeg and draw off the heat. Add 3 tablespoons of the sauce to the chopped spinach in the food processor bowl and buzz to a purée. Stir all but 1 tablespoon of the grated cheese into the remaining sauce.

**3** Spoon the spinach purée into a buttered 1.1 litre (2 pint) gratin dish and spread level. Separate the eggs, cracking the whites into a mixing bowl and stirring the yolks into the cheese sauce. Whisk the egg whites to stiff peaks and fold into the cheese sauce. Spoon the mixture over the spinach layer and spread level. Sprinkle with the remaining grated cheese. Refrigerate until required.

**4** Heat the oven to 160°C (325°F or gas no. 3). Set the spinach and cheese gratin in the heated oven and bake for 35–40 minutes or until the mixture is thoroughly hot and the top glazed and golden. Serve from the baking dish.

# Baked Garlic-Stuffed Mushrooms

**1** Peel the mushrooms and remove the stalks. Set aside 4 mushrooms and chop the remainder finely.

**2** Melt the butter in a large frying pan. Add the chopped mushrooms and cook gently until they are well softened and the juices have evaporated – about 10 minutes. Add a seasoning of salt and pepper. Stir for a moment and draw off the heat.

**3** Buzz the bread slices and parsley heads in a food processor. Turn into a mixing bowl. Add the finely grated lemon rind and the garlic pressed through a crusher. Turn the mushroom mixture into the bowl. Stir to mix. Fill the reserved mushrooms with the stuffing mixture pressing it in firmly. Cover and chill until required.

**4** Heat the oven to 190°C (375°F or gas no. 5). Arrange mushrooms on a lightly oiled baking tray. Set in the heated oven and bake for 15 minutes until hot, then serve with a little extra melted butter drizzled over and a sprig of flat leaf parsley alongside.

8 large flat mushrooms
50 g (2 oz) butter
salt and freshly milled pepper
50 g (2 oz) slices white bread,
  crusts removed
25 g (1 oz) fresh parsley
grated rind ½ lemon
3 cloves garlic
melted butter to serve
fresh flat leaf parsley sprigs
  to garnish

**Serves 4**
Preparation time: 40 minutes
Cooking time: 15 minutes

# Asparagus with Egg and Melted Butter Sauce

*This is good as a starter or a light main dish. Serve with hot French bread to mop up the juices.*

**1** Carefully wash the asparagus, then trim the stalks to the same length, cutting off the woody base. Bring the eggs to the boil from cold and simmer for 4 minutes to soft boil, then drain and shell.

**2** Drop the asparagus into a saucepan of boiling salted water large enough for the stalks to lie flat. Cover with the pan lid and simmer gently for 8 minutes – test by piercing a stalk with a knife tip. When ready, scoop the asparagus from the pan with two forks or a slotted spoon and drain well on a clean tea cloth (water droplets will dilute the dressing).

**3** Meanwhile, melt the butter over a low heat, let it settle for a moment then slowly pour it off into a container to clarify, leaving the milky sediment behind. Rinse the saucepan and return the butter, adding the chives and freshly milled pepper. Warm through.

**4** Arrange the asparagus on individual warmed plates, together with a halved soft-boiled egg and a spoonful of butter sauce. Serve the remaining sauce separately.

700–900 g (1½–2 lb) fresh
  asparagus
4 eggs
100 g (4 oz) butter
2 tablespoons chopped
  fresh chives
freshly milled pepper

**Serves 4**
Preparation time: 25 minutes
Cooking time: 8–10 minutes

# Parma Ham with Nectarines in a Mint Vinaigrette

**1** In a mixing bowl, pound the mint with the sugar (use a wooden spoon) to draw out the flavouring oils. Add a seasoning of salt and pepper, the raspberry or red wine vinegar and stir to dissolve the sugar. Stir in the olive oil and taste for flavour – the dressing should be sweet-sharp.

**2** Cut the nectarines in half, following the natural line, and twist the halves to separate. Remove the stones. Add the nectarines to the dressing and turn to coat them. Marinate until serving time.

**3** Arrange the nectarine halves with a spoonful of dressing on six plates. Add slices of Parma ham and serve.

2 tablespoons chopped
  fresh mint
1 teaspoon caster sugar
salt and freshly milled pepper
2 tablespoons raspberry or
  red wine vinegar
6 tablespoons olive oil
3 ripe nectarines
12 slices Parma ham

**Serves 6**
Preparation time: 10 minutes,
  plus marinating time

# Individual Smoked Salmon Tarts

**1** Lightly grease 6 fluted tart tins, 7.5 cm (3 inches) in diameter. On a floured surface roll the pastry out thinly. Using a 10 cm (4 inch) round cutter, stamp out 6 circles of pastry and use them to line the prepared tins. Refrigerate the pastry cases while preparing the smoked salmon filling.

**2** In a medium mixing bowl combine the crème fraîche, a seasoning of salt and freshly milled pepper and the eggs. Shred the slices of smoked salmon with two forks and add the shreds to the mixture.

**3** Heat the oven to 200°C (400°F or gas no. 6) and set a baking tray in the oven to heat up. Spoon the filling into the pastry cases making sure the smoked salmon pieces are evenly disributed. Sprinkle with the grated Parmesan cheese. Set the tarts directly on the hot baking tray, return to the oven and bake for 15–20 minutes or until they are well risen and golden.

**4** Set a tart on each of six serving plates, add a watercress garnish and drizzle the vinaigrette over the watercress.

shortcrust pastry made using
  175 g (6 oz) plain flour and
  75 g (3 oz) butter
6–8 watercress sprigs
1–2 tablespoons oil and
  vinegar dressing
FOR THE FILLING:
1 x 200 ml tub crème fraîche
salt and freshly milled pepper
2 eggs
100 g (4 oz) sliced smoked
  salmon
2 tablespoons grated
  Parmesan cheese

**Serves 6**
Preparation time: 20–25 minutes
Cooking time: 15–20 minutes

# Baked Oysters with Garlic and Herb Buttered Crumbs

*Place the baked oysters in the centre of the table as soon as they come from the oven, then let guests help themselves – it looks dramatic.*

12 fresh oysters
rock salt for baking
50 g (2 oz) fresh white
  breadcrumbs
25 g (1 oz) fresh parsley
grated rind 1 lemon
2 cloves garlic
100 g (4 oz) butter

**Serves 4**
Preparation time: 25–30 minutes
Cooking time: 5 minutes

**1** You need the right blunt-tipped, strong oyster knife to prise open the shells, otherwise have the oysters opened by your fishmonger. He will arrange them in the deep half shells for you – carry them home carefully to avoid spilling the precious juices.

**2** Spread a layer of rock salt in an ovenproof baking or gratin dish using 1 or 2 dishes to contain all the oysters. Arrange the oysters, pressing them into the salt to hold them steady.

**3** Buzz the breadcrumbs and parsley heads in a food processor. Turn into a mixing bowl, add the finely grated lemon rind and the garlic, pressed through a garlic crusher. Melt the butter and stir into the mixture with a fork.

**4** Heat the oven to 200°C (400°F or gas no. 6). Spoon the garlic and herb buttered crumbs into each oyster shell. Set the oysters in the heated oven and bake for 5 minutes. Serve at once.

## FABULOUS FINGER FOOD

Shop-bought, ready-baked, bite-sized pastry cups or croustades, are handy for drinks party nibbles. I always have a couple of boxes handy. Just spoon in any one, or more of these flavoursome mixtures and serve:
• Seasoned cream cheese and smoked salmon trimmings
• Taramasalata with finely chopped spring onions
• Mushrooms fried in garlic butter
• Houmous with a sprinkling of paprika
• Scrambled egg with lumpfish caviar
• Soured cream and dill pickled herrings
• Cold cooked prawns in your favourite mayonnaise

# Potato Pancakes with Caviar and Crème Fraîche

*Make the potato pancakes ahead, then reheat for serving and make sure everything else is well chilled.*

**1** Peel the potatoes and grate finely – using the finest shredder on a food processor is the quickest and best way. Cover the potato shreds with cold water, add the lemon juice and leave to soak for 30 minutes.

**2** Peel and grate the onion finely. In a mixing bowl, combine the grated onion, flour, baking powder, egg and a seasoning of salt and pepper. Mix to a soft batter. Drain the potato shreds and squeeze dry by pressing them in your hands. Add to the batter and mix well.

**3** Heat 2–3 tablespoons olive oil in a 25 cm (10 inch) frying pan. Drop in tablespoons of the potato mixture (not more than 2–3 at a time) and flatten them slightly. Fry for 2–3 minutes until golden on the underside, then flip them over to brown the second side. Transfer to a baking tray.

**4** Continue with the remaining batter until it is all used up – you should get about 20 potato pancakes. These can be prepared ahead, then reheated on the baking tray in a hot oven 190°C (375°F or gas no. 5) for 4–5 minutes.

**5** Serve the hot potato pancakes with chilled caviar and spoonfuls of crème fraîche.

700 g (1½ lb) baking potatoes
juice 1 lemon
1 small onion
2 tablespoons plain flour
1 teaspoon baking powder
1 egg
salt and freshly milled pepper
olive oil for frying
2 x 100 g jars lumpfish caviar
1 x 500 ml tub crème fraîche

**Serves 4**
Preparation time: 20 minutes,
  plus soaking time
Cooking time: 15–20 minutes

# Watercress Mousse

2 x 75 g packets watercress
2 x 225 g cartons curd cheese
salt and freshly milled pepper
grated nutmeg
150 ml (¼ pint) vegetable stock
1 tablespoon powdered
  gelatine
150 ml (¼ pint) double cream
FOR THE DRESSING:
4 tablespoons olive oil
1 tablespoon white wine vinegar
pinch of sugar
salt and freshly milled pepper
6 black olives to garnish

**Serves 6**

Preparation time: 35 minutes, plus
  chilling time

**1** Chop the watercress leaves finely in a food processor, setting aside 1-2 leafy tops for a garnish. Add the curd cheese, a good seasoning of salt and freshly milled pepper and a grating of nutmeg. Cover and blend. Turn the mixture into a mixing bowl.

**2** Measure 3 tablespoons of the vegetable stock into a saucepan. Sprinkle in the gelatine and allow to soften for a few moments. Set over a low heat and stir until the gelatine has dissolved. Draw off the heat and stir in the remaining stock.

**3** Stir the warm stock (with gelatine dissolved) into the watercress and curd cheese blend; mix well. Arrange 6 x 150 ml (¼ pint) pudding moulds on a baking tray.

**4** Whip the cream to soft peaks and fold into the mixture. Divide the watercress mousse between the moulds. Transfer to the refrigerator and chill for at least 4 hours or overnight.

**5** To make the dressing, combine the olive oil, vinegar, sugar and a seasoning of salt and pepper.

**6** Unmould and arrange the mousses on individual plates. Garnish each one with the reserved watercress leaves. Spoon a little of the dressing over each mousse and add a black olive to garnish.

# Warm Salad of Pheasant with Herb Leaves and a Balsamic Vinegar Dressing

2 thick slices white bread
3 tablespoons olive oil
2 pheasant breasts
1 x 60 g packet herb salad
  leaves
FOR THE DRESSING:
5 tablespoons olive oil
1 tablespoon balsamic vinegar
½ teaspoon herbes de Provence
salt and freshly milled pepper

**Serves 3–4**

Preparation time: 15 minutes
Cooking time: 10–12 minutes

**1** Cut the crusts off the bread slices and discard. Then cut the bread into small cubes. Heat 2 tablespoons of the olive oil in a frying pan. Add the bread cubes and fry 1–2 minutes, stirring until they are crisp and brown. Lift out and drain on absorbent kitchen paper. (Alternatively, buy in the croûtons, if you like.)

**2** Add the remaining olive oil to the frying pan and add the pheasant breasts. Fry over a moderate heat turning them to seal and brown both sides for 6–8 minutes, until cooked but still a little pink in the middle. Lift from the pan but save the pan drippings.

**3** Turn the herb salad leaves into a bowl. Combine the olive oil, balsamic vinegar, herbs and a seasoning of salt and milled pepper for the dressing. Add 1 tablespoon of the dressing to the herb leaves and toss them. Add the croûtons to the herb leaves. Pour the remaining dressing into the pan drippings, bring to a simmer, stirring.

**4** Carve the pheasant breasts in thin slices. Divide the herb salad leaves between 3–4 serving plates. Arrange pheasant slices on top. Spoon over the warm dressing and serve.

# Pastry Tartlets with Two Fillings

*If you prefer to offer only one choice, just double up on one of the fillings.*

225 g (8 oz) plain flour

150 g (5 oz) butter

1 egg yolk

**PRAWNS IN GARLIC BUTTER:**

75 g (3 oz) butter

2 cloves garlic

225 g (8 oz) cooked and
  peeled king prawns

salt and freshly milled pepper

1 tablespoon chopped fresh
  parsley

**MUSHROOMS IN BRANDY
CREAM:**

225 g (8 oz) oyster
  mushrooms

25 g (1 oz) butter

1 tablespoon brandy

150 ml (¼ pint) double cream

salt and freshly milled pepper

**Serves 8**

Preparation time: 35 minutes,
  plus chilling time
Cooking time: 15 minutes

**1** Sift the flour into a mixing bowl. Add the butter in pieces and rub in with your fingertips. Mix the egg yolk with 2 tablespoons of cold water in a cup. Add to the dry ingredients and mix with your fingertips to make a dough. Turn onto a floured work surface and knead until smooth. Chill for 30 minutes.

**2** Heat the oven to 190°C (375°F or gas no. 5). Roll the pastry out thinly and, with a floured 7.5 cm (3 inch) round cutter, stamp out 8 circles of pastry, using all the trimmings. Press the circles over the upturned bases of 8 deep tartlet or bun tins. Prick each with a fork. Arrange on a baking tray and set in the heated oven for 12–15 minutes. Lift off and cool on a wire rack. These will keep for 24 hours in a lidded tin. Warm in a slow oven before filling.

**3** For the prawns in garlic butter: melt the butter in a large frying pan. Add the crushed garlic and stir. Add the prawns and turn in the hot butter. Season with salt and pepper to taste and stir in the freshly chopped parsley.

**4** For the mushrooms in brandy cream: leave the mushrooms whole or halve them if large. Melt the butter in a frying pan. Add the mushrooms and sauté for a few minutes to soften. Transfer to a plate. Add the brandy to the pan, let it bubble up, then pour in the cream and bring to the boil. Return the mushrooms to the pan, add seasoning and then heat through to warm.

**5** Arrange the pastry shells on a warmed plate. Spoon the prawns in garlic butter into half the shells and the mushrooms in brandy cream into the remainder, and serve.

# Best-Dressed Avocados

First, make sure the avocados are ripe. To open, run a sharp knife round the equator and twist to separate. Slash the stone with a knife, then twist to lift the stone away. This saves messy 'digging in' with fingertips. Simply serve with lemon juice squeezed over and freshly milled pepper. Alternatively, spoon one of the following dressings into each half. Recipes sufficient for 6 avocado halves.

**Honey, Mustard and Thyme Dressing:** Combine 3 tablespoons red wine vinegar, 2 tablespoons coarsegrain mustard, a seasoning of salt and pepper, 2 tablespoons clear honey and 100 ml (4 fl oz) olive oil and mix. Add 1 tablespoon crumbled fresh thyme leaves.

**Sliced Strawberry and Mint Dressing:** Pound 2 tablespoons chopped fresh mint leaves with 1 level teaspoon caster sugar to draw the juices. Add a seasoning of salt and pepper, 2 tablespoons raspberry vinegar and stir to dissolve the seasoning. Add 4 tablespoons olive oil and 225 g (8 oz) sliced fresh strawberries.

**Diced Tomato and Herb Dressing:** Skin 3 tomatoes, deseed and finely dice. Place in a bowl, add 1 teaspoon caster sugar, a seasoning of salt and freshly milled pepper and 50 ml (2 fl oz) red wine vinegar. Marinate for 1 hour. Stir in 100 ml (4 fl oz) olive oil and 1 tablespoon chopped fresh tarragon leaves.

**Soured Cream and Chive Dressing:** Combine 3 tablespoons soured cream with 4 tablespoons prepared oil and vinegar dressing, and mix to an emulsion. Add 2 tablespoons finely chopped fresh chives.

**Orange with Ginger Dressing:** Cut the peel and pith from 2 oranges, then cut the flesh into chunks. Mash 2 pieces stem ginger. Combine 3 tablespoons white wine vinegar, 2 tablespoons stem ginger syrup, 1 tablespoon soft brown sugar and 100 ml (4 fl oz) olive oil, then add the orange and the mashed stem ginger.

**Serves 6**

Preparation time: 10–15 minutes, plus marinating time, where applicable

# Black Olive Polenta

**1** Add the salt to 600 ml (1 pint) cold water, bring to the boil, then simmer. Add polenta steadily, sirring continuously. Bring to the boil and cook for 5 minutes until smooth and thick, stirring often.

**2** Draw off the heat, season with pepper and add the chopped olives. Turn mixture onto a plate. Leave to cool and set.

**3** Cut polenta into thick 1 cm (½ inch) slices. Arrange on a baking tray, brush with a mixture of the melted butter and olive oil. Grill for about 5 minutes until warmed. Turn, brush again and grill the other side for 2–3 minutes, then serve.

**Sun-Dried Tomato Polenta:** Stir in 25 g (1 oz) chopped sun-dried tomatoes (in oil) and ½ teaspoon dried oregano instead of the olives.

**Sage Polenta:** Stir 50 g (2 oz) grated Parmesan cheese and 5–6 fresh sage leaves, chopped, into the hot polenta in place of the black olives.

1 teaspoon salt
100 g (4 oz) instant polenta
freshly milled pepper
12 black olives, pitted and
  coarsely chopped
25 g (1 oz) melted butter
2 tablespoons olive oil

**Serves 4**
Preparation time: 15 minutes,
  plus cooling time
Cooking time: 5 minutes

---

## Katie's Tip
You can add toppings to slices of polenta to make it into a supper or lunch snack. All the delicious things you'd choose for a pizza will also go on polenta.

---

# Mozzarella Garlic Bread

*Cheese melts over the surface of this delicious variation on the more usual garlic bread; cut across the bread, in chunky pieces, for serving.*

**1** Measure the butter (at room temperature) into a food processor bowl. Peel and crush the garlic with the salt. Add the oil and mashed garlic to the butter. Cover and mix to a soft blend. Add the parsley and a seasoning of pepper and mix using the on/off switch. Or, beat all the ingredients in a mixing bowl with a wooden spoon.

**2** Split the baguettes in half lengthways. Spread the cut side of each half with the garlic butter. Cut the mozzarella cheese in 5 mm (¼ inch) slices and arrange over the garlic buttered surface. Cover and chill until required.

**3** Heat the oven to 190°C (375°F or gas no. 5). Arrange the bread on a baking tray – a piece of crinkled foil will stop them from tipping over. Set in the heated oven and bake for 10 minutes or until bubbling hot.

100 g (4 oz) unsalted butter
3 cloves garlic
½ teaspoon salt
2 tablespoons olive oil
2 tablespoons chopped parsley
freshly milled pepper
250 g (9 oz) mozzarella cheese
2 small baguettes

**Serves 4–6**
Preparation time: 10 minutes,
  plus chilling time
Cooking time: 10 minutes

# Bruschetta with Toppings

2 plum tomatoes
1 x 150 g packet Italian
   mozzarella cheese
1 x 50 g tin anchovy fillets
100 g (4 oz) goat's cheese
4 thick slices country bread,
   preferably Italian such as
   Pugliese
1 clove garlic
1–2 tablespoons olive oil
Tapenade (recipe below)

**Serves 4**

Preparation time: 10 minutes
Cooking time: 3–4 minutes

**1** Slice the tomatoes and cut the mozzarella into thin slices. Drain the anchovies and cut the goat's cheese into small wedges.

**2** Grill the bread slices on both sides. Rub the cut garlic clove lightly over one side of each slice and drizzle with olive oil. Cut each slice in half to make 8 bruschetta.

**3** Top four bruschetta with tomato slices, then mozzarella slices, then anchovies. Spread the remaining four with Tapenade and top with goat's cheese.

**4** Arrange the bruschetta on a baking tray and grill until the toppings are bubbling. Serve hot with a crisp green salad.

**Tapenade:** In a food processor, combine 100 g (4 oz) pitted black olives, 4–5 anchovy fillets, 1 teaspoon Dijon mustard, freshly milled pepper to taste, 1 tablespoon lemon juice and 2 peeled garlic cloves. Cover and buzz to a purée. With the motor running, add 75 ml (3 fl oz) olive oil and mix to a coarse purée. Spoon into a screw-topped jar and store in the refrigerator for up to 3 months.

# Feta Cheese Filos

**1** Prepare the filling first. Cut the feta cheese into small dice. Trim and rinse the spring onions, then chop all the white and some of the green stems. Turn the curd cheese into a mixing bowl, add a seasoning of salt and pepper and beat until smooth and soft. Stir in the diced feta cheese and the chopped spring onions.

**2** On a work surface, stack the filo sheets and cover with a damp cloth. Combine the butter and oil in a saucepan and heat to melt. Taking one filo sheet at a time, brush with the melted butter mixture, then fold the sheet in half lengthways. Brush with melted butter again. Place a heaped teaspoonful of the filling 1 cm (½ inch) in from the short end. Fold a corner of the pastry in over the filling to form a triangle. Turn the triangle over and over (keeping the edges straight) to the end of the pastry strip. Repeat with remaining filling and pastry. Brush filos with melted butter. Cover and refrigerate until nearer serving time.

**3** Heat the oven to 190°C (375°F or gas no. 5). Let the prepared filos return to room temperature, then arrange them on greased baking trays. Bake in the oven for 10–12 minutes or until crisp and brown. Dust with paprika and serve warm.

200 g (7 oz) feta cheese
1 bunch (6–8) spring onions
225 g (8 oz) curd cheese
salt and freshly milled pepper
1 x 200 g packet fresh filo
  pastry
50 g (2 oz) butter
1 tablespoon vegetable oil
paprika for dusting

**Makes 25**
Preparation time: 30 minutes,
  plus chilling time
Cooking time: 10–12 minutes

# Sesame Prawn Toasts

**1** If prawns are frozen allow them to thaw and discard the juices. Put prawns in a food processor bowl. Add the snipped bacon rashers, spring onion, fresh ginger, salt, egg white and cornflour. Blend to a smooth paste.

**2** Spread bread slices thickly with the prawn mixture. Trim and discard crusts. Spread sesame seeds on a plate and dip bread slices (prawn side down) in the sesame seeds. Press firmly, coating slices evenly. Cover and chill bread slices for 1 hour.

**3** Cut each bread slice crossways to make 4 triangles.

**4** Pour sufficient oil into a frying pan to cover the base by at least 2.5 cm (1 inch). Set over a moderate heat and when hot, slide in bread pieces, sesame seed side down, and fry until golden turning to brown both sides. You will have to fry these in batches. Drain sesame prawn toasts on absorbent kitchen paper.

200 g (7 oz) cooked and
  peeled prawns
2 unsmoked streaky bacon
  rashers
1 tablespoon chopped spring
  onion
1 teaspoon grated fresh ginger
¼ teaspoon salt
1 egg white
1 tablespoon cornflour
6 thin slices white bread
2–3 tablespoons sesame seeds
grapeseed oil for frying

**Makes 24**
Preparation time: 30 minutes,
  plus chilling time
Cooking time: 10 minutes

# Croustades

*Use a sliced loaf to make these crunchy finger rolls, which you can prepare ahead, then bake. Garlic butter makes a delicious alternative to the filling I've used below.*

12 thin slices white bread
100 g (4 oz) butter
100 g (4 oz) Roquefort cheese
TO FINISH:
50 g (2 oz) melted butter
2 teaspoons caraway seeds

**Makes 24**

Preparation time: 25 minutes,
  plus chilling time
Cooking time: 15 minutes

**1** Cut away the crusts from the bread – the quickest way is to cut the slices in small stacks. Then roll each slice with a rolling pin to flatten it.

**2** In a mixing bowl cream the butter (at room temperature) and the Roquefort cheese until they are softened and well mixed. Spread the Roquefort butter on each bread slice right into the edges. Roll slices up tightly, then cut each one in half across the centre. Grease a 28 x 18 cm (11 x 7 inch) Swiss roll or baking tin (with edges) with a little melted butter. Pack in the bread rolls tightly, with the ends of the slices underneath. Cover and refrigerate for at least several hours or overnight.

**3** Heat the oven to 200°C (400°F or gas no. 6). Brush each roll with the remaining melted butter. Sprinkle with the caraway seeds. Bake in the oven for 15 minutes or until golden and crisp. Serve warm.

# Butterfly Prawns

1 x 250 g packet frozen raw
  tiger prawns
3 tablespoons grapeseed oil
1 tablespoon clear honey
1 tablespoon hot chilli sauce
1 tablespoon lemon juice
pinch of five spice powder

**Makes 15**

Preparation time: 15 minutes,
  plus marinating time
Cooking time: 3–4 minutes

**1** Allow the prawns to thaw and discard the juices. Using forefingers and thumbs, pull open the prawn shells and peel them off leaving the tail intact. Slit along the back with a knife to open and remove the black vein.

**2** Combine the oil, honey, chilli sauce, lemon juice and five spice powder in a mixing bowl. Add the prawns and stir to coat, then refrigerate and leave to marinate for 4 hours.

**3** Heat the grill to hot and set the grill rack 7.5 cm (3 inches) from the heat source. Lift the prawns from the marinade with a fork and spread the prawns on a baking sheet. Set under the heated grill for 3–4 minutes, turning them over. When ready the flesh will firm up and turn pink and the back will open out. Set prawns on a platter, guests can pick them up by the tail end.

# Smoked Salmon with Sushi Rice

**1** Start with the sushi rice. Wash the rice grains in cold water then drain. Put the rice and 200 ml (7 fl oz) cold water into a saucepan and soak for 30 minutes. Then bring the rice to the boil, stirring. Lower the heat, cover the pan and cook the rice for about 15 minutes or until the grains are tender and the water has been absorbed. Remove from the heat and let stand for a further 10–15 minutes, covered with pan lid.

**2** Meanwhile measure the cider vinegar, sugar and salt into a saucepan. Bring to a simmer, stirring to dissolve the sugar and draw off the heat. Turn the cooked rice into a bowl, sprinkle over the vinegar mixture and fork through the rice.

**3** Separate the smoked salmon slices and cut lengthways into strips approximately 2.5 x 7.5 cm (1 x 3 inches). Take teaspoonfuls of the sushi rice and press into a ball, then flatten out on a smoked salmon piece and roll or fold closed into a parcel.

**4** Using the tip of a sharp knife slice the leek leaves lengthways into long fine strips – like string. Scald the leek strips in boiling water for 2–3 minutes, then drain and cover them with cold water. Take the leek strips and tie attractively around the smoked salmon parcels. Let the tails trail, only snipping them if they are too long.

225 g (8 oz) smoked salmon
2–3 green leek leaves
FOR THE SUSHI RICE:
100 g (4 oz) round grain
  (pudding) rice
2 tablespoons cider vinegar
1 tablespoon caster sugar
1 teaspoon salt

**Makes 24**
Preparation time: 40 minutes,
  plus soaking and cooling time
Cooking time: 15 minutes

# Marinated Olives

**1** Rinse bottled or tinned unstuffed black and green olives and place in glass jars. Add fresh thyme sprigs, slivers of garlic and thin wedges of lemon. Add olive oil to cover and let the olives marinate for a week.

# Mushroom Cups with Cream Cheese

18–20 closed cup mushrooms
100 g (4 oz) soft cream cheese
½ small onion, peeled
salt and freshly milled pepper
1 x 100 g jar lumpfish caviar

**Makes 18–20**
Preparation time: 25 minutes

**1** Discard stalks and pick over the mushroom cups. Brush clean, but do not wash them. Take a sliver from the top of each mushroom so they will sit steady. In a bowl beat the cream cheese to soften.
**2** Grate the onion on to a plate to get onion juice and some fine grated onion. Beat sufficient grated onion into the cheese to get a mild flavour, then season. An alternative would be to trim and finely chop a bunch of spring onions and add these instead. Fill the mushroom caps with small teaspoons of the mixture, then top with lumpfish caviar.

# Chicken Satays

3 tablespoons dark soy sauce
3 tablespoons smooth peanut
  butter
1 tablespoon lemon juice
1 teaspoon hot chilli sauce
75 ml (3 fl oz) grapeseed oil
2 cloves garlic
3 chicken breasts
100 g (4 oz) dry roasted
  peanuts

**Makes 24**
Preparation time: 15 minutes,
  plus marinating time
Cooking time: 5–6 minutes

**1** Combine the dark soy sauce, peanut butter, lemon juice, chilli sauce and grapeseed oil in a mixing bowl. Peel and crush the garlic and add to the mixture.
**2** Remove the chicken skin and cut the chicken flesh lengthways and across into bite-sized pieces. Add to the marinade and stir well. Cover and refrigerate for 4 hours. Buzz the dry roasted peanuts in a blender or food processor to finely chop.
**3** Heat the grill to hot and set the grill rack 7.5 cm (3 inches) from the heat source. Lift the pieces of chicken from the marinade and spread on a baking tray. Set under the heated grill for 5–6 minutes stirring up the chicken pieces as they cook.
**4** To serve, stab pieces of chicken on cocktail sticks. Roll in dry roasted peanuts.

# Tutti Frutti Chocolate Truffles

*A heavenly mouthful – dried apricots, raisins and walnuts with chocolate.*

**1** Break the chocolate into a medium mixing bowl. Set over a saucepan half-filled with hot water (off the heat) until melted.
**2** Scissor snip the apricots and place them in a food processor bowl, add the walnut pieces, seedless raisins, grated orange rind and the liqueur. Cover and process until the mixture is finely chopped.
**3** Add the chopped fruit and nuts to the melted chocolate and stir to mix. Take teaspoons of the mixture, form into walnut-sized balls and set on waxed paper. Chill until set firm.

1 x 150 g bar plain chocolate
100 g (4 oz) ready-to-eat
  dried apricots
100 g (4 oz) walnut pieces
100 g (4 oz) seedless raisins
grated rind 1 orange
2 teaspoons Grand Marnier
  liqueur

**Makes 30**
Preparation time: 20 minutes

## PERFECT CHEESE SOUFFLÉ

Heat the oven to 190°C (375°F or gas no. 5). Butter 6 soufflé dishes or ramekins, scatter grated Parmesan cheese inside. Set the dishes on a baking tray. Warm 300 ml (½ pint) milk with a bay leaf and a thick slice of onion. Infuse for 5 minutes. Melt 50 g (2 oz) butter in a saucepan, then stir in 40 g (1½ oz) flour and cook gently 1–2 minutes. Gradually pour in the infused milk, beating well. Simmer gently for 3–4 minutes, then draw off the heat. Add seasoning, a grating of nutmeg, 50 g (2 oz) grated Gruyère cheese and 50 g (2 oz) grated Parmesan. Stir until the cheese melts. Turn mixture into a mixing bowl and cool until lukewarm. Stir in 4 egg yolks. Taste for flavour. Whisk egg whites to stiff folds (don't overbeat). Fold in a third of the beaten whites first – then the rest. Pour into the prepared dishes, filling them halfway. Set in the oven and bake for 20 minutes until risen and golden.

# Light Lunches or Suppers

Cheese, eggs, vegetables and rice are the basics of most suppers. Cheese is a quick and instantly delicious flavour to use in recipes and here, too, are up-to-date main meals with vegetables. Good suppers should be easy to prepare, and even better when they can be served straight from the baking dish – just the kind of food to share round the kitchen table.

*Couscous with Skewered Vegetables*

# Couscous with Skewered Vegetables

4 medium courgettes

6 parsnips

450 g (1 lb) cherry tomatoes

3 tablespoons olive oil

2 tablespoons clear honey

2 tablespoons dark soy sauce

½ teaspoon salt

225 g (8 oz) couscous

25 g (1 oz) butter

50 g (2 oz) toasted pine
    kernels

Red Pepper Sauce to serve
    (recipe below)

**Serves 4**

Preparation time: 15 minutes

Cooking time: 25 minutes

**1** Trim the courgettes and pare some of the green skin, then cut across in 2.5 cm (1 inch) thick slices. Pare the parsnips, discard thin root tips and cut the parsnips into chunky pieces. Place the pieces in cold water, bring to the boil and simmer for 8 minutes until barely tender, then drain.

**2** Spear the cherry tomatoes, courgette pieces and parsnip chunks onto bamboo skewers – spear vegetables of a kind and aim for 4 skewers of each vegetable. Combine 2 tablespoons of the olive oil with the honey and the soy sauce to make a baste.

**3** Put 400 ml (¾ pint) cold water, the salt and remaining olive oil into a pan. Bring to the boil. Remove from the heat and stir in the couscous. Cover and let the couscous stand for at least 5 minutes.

**4** Meanwhile, heat the grill to hot. Line the grill rack with kitchen foil and set it 7.5 cm (3 inches) from the heat source. Brush the kebabs with the honey and soy sauce baste and arrange on the grill rack. Cook for about 8–10 minutes, turning several times and brushing with the flavoured baste.

**5** Add the butter to the couscous and fork through to separate the grains. Turn onto a serving platter and add the vegetable skewers. Or, using a fork, run the vegetables off the skewers onto the couscous base. Sprinkle with toasted pine kernels and serve with Red Pepper Sauce.

**Red Pepper Sauce:** Halve, seed and quarter 2 red sweet peppers. Brush with olive oil and grill both sides until the skin is blackened. Cool and pull off the skins. Put the pepper pieces in a food processor bowl with 1 peeled clove of garlic and a seasoning of salt and pepper. Cover and buzz to a purée. Add 100 ml (4 fl oz) olive oil and a dash of Tabasco sauce and buzz again. Store in a screw-topped jar – it will keep for ages.

## Katie's Tip

The method above is a particularly quick and easy way to prepare couscous. You can use it any time with lamb tagine, for example, or a fish dish with a spicy sauce. I like to serve it with game casseroles that have a rich gravy. Vary the flavour of couscous by using an appropriate stock instead of water, or by stirring in a flavoured garlic or herb butter.

# Gruyère Cheese Croquettes with Lemon

1 Melt half the butter in a saucepan over a low heat. Stir in the flour and cook gently for 1 minute. Gradually stir in the milk. Bring to the boil, stirring to make a smooth, thick sauce. Simmer for 2–3 minutes and draw off the heat.

2 Add the grated cheese, a seasoning of salt and pepper and a grating of nutmeg. Stir until the cheese has melted. Separate the egg, reserving the white on a plate, and stir the yolk into the cheese mixture. Leave for 2 hours until quite cold.

3 With wet fingers, shape the mixture into 12 small croquettes. Mix the egg white with a fork to break it up. Dip each croquette in the egg white then in the toasted breadcrumbs. Chill for at least 1 hour.

4 Melt the rest of the butter in a large frying pan over a moderate heat. Add the croquettes and fry, turning once, until brown all over. Serve on toast with lemon wedges for squeezing.

100 g (4 oz) butter
50 g (2 oz) flour
300 ml (½ pint) milk
100 g (4 oz) grated Gruyère
   cheese
salt and freshly milled pepper
grated nutmeg
1 egg
toasted breadcrumbs for
   coating
4 slices toast
lemon wedges to serve

**Serves 4**

Preparation time: 25 minutes,
   plus chilling time
Cooking time: 10 minutes

# Cheddar Cheese and Apple Strata

1 Remove the crusts from the bread and cut the slices in half. Peel and finely chop the onion. Peel, core and dice the apple. Grate the Cheddar cheese.

2 Heat the butter in a frying pan, add the onion and cook until soft but not brown. Add the diced apple, stir and draw off the heat.

3 Arrange 6 bread halves in a buttered 1.7 litre (3 pint) soufflé dish. Cover with the grated cheese, spoon over the onion and apple mixture. Top with the remaining bread slices.

4 Whisk the eggs, milk, mustard and season with salt and freshly milled pepper. Pour over the bread slices. Sprinkle with paprika. Refrigerate for 1 hour or overnight.

5 Heat the oven to 180°C (350°F or gas no. 4). Set the dish in the heated oven and bake uncovered for 45–50 minutes or until puffy and brown. Allow to rest for 5 minutes, spoon out and serve.

6 slices day-old bread
1 medium onion
1 tart dessert apple
175 g (6 oz) mature Cheddar
   cheese
25 g (1 oz) butter
3 eggs
300 ml (½ pint) milk
1 teaspoon Dijon mustard
salt and freshly milled pepper
paprika for sprinkling

**Serves 3**

Preparation time: 20 minutes,
   plus standing time
Cooking time: 50 minutes

# Risotto with Stir-Fried Asparagus

**1** Peel and finely chop the onion. Heat the oil in a large 25 cm (10 inch) frying pan, add the onion and cook gently over a medium heat to soften.

**2** Add the rice, stirring to coat the grains with the oil and onion and cook for a further 2 minutes. Stir in 300 ml (½ pint) of the hot stock and allow the risotto to cook gently uncovered. As the liquid is absorbed by the rice, add the remaining stock and the vermouth, about ¼ pint at a time. Stir the mixture frequently to loosen the rice grains – they will be tender by the time the liquid is absorbed – about 25–30 minutes.

**3** Meanwhile trim the woody base away from each asparagus stem. Line up several stalks on a cutting board and using a sharp kitchen knife cut across the asparagus on the diagonal to make slanting slices about 2.5 cm (1 inch) long, taking in the heads and stalks.

**4** Melt the butter in a separate frying pan, add the asparagus and stir-fry over a moderate heat until tender crisp, 3–4 minutes.

**5** Draw the pan of risotto off the heat. Turn the asparagus and butter into the risotto and gently fork through. Add Parmesan shavings and serve.

1 medium onion
2 tablespoons olive oil
225 g (8 oz) risotto rice
600 ml (1 pint) vegetable stock
100 ml (4 fl oz) dry white vermouth
50 g (2 oz) butter
450 g (1 lb) asparagus spears
2 tablespoons Parmesan cheese shavings

**Serves 3**
Preparation time: 10 minutes
Cooking time: 40 minutes

# Courgette and Feta Cheese Risotto

**1** Peel and finely chop the onion. Heat the oil in a large 25 cm (10 inch) frying pan (with a lid), stir in the onion and cook, covered, over a low heat until soft but not browned. Add the rice and stir to mix. Add about half of the stock, cook gently, uncovered, for 15 minutes.

**2** Trim and slice the courgettes. Add to a pan of boiling salted water and bring back to the boil. Turn into a colander and drain well.

**3** Stir the remaining stock and vermouth into the partly cooked rice. Place the courgettes on top. Cover with the pan lid and cook for a further 10–15 minutes, or until the vegetables and rice are tender and the liquid is completely absorbed.

**4** Break the feta cheese into large crumbly pieces, then scatter over the rice and vegetables. Stir and heat the mixture for about 2 minutes more, then sprinkle the chopped tarragon over and serve immediately.

1 medium onion
1 tablespoon olive oil
225 g (8 oz) risotto rice
600 ml (1 pint) vegetable stock
4 medium courgettes
100 ml (4 fl oz) dry white vermouth
1 x 200 g packet feta cheese
2 tablespoons chopped fresh tarragon

**Serves 4**
Preparation time: 10 minutes
Cooking time: 35 minutes

# Date, Ricotta Cheese and Filo Tart

*Fresh dates from the Jordan River Valley are in the supermarkets. They are not overly sweet and are marvellous in savoury tarts or salads.*

6 sheets fresh filo pastry

50 g (2 oz) butter

1 tablespoon olive oil

200 g (7 oz) fresh dates

50 g (2 oz) toasted pine
  kernels

3 eggs

300 ml (½ pint) single cream

1 x 250 g tub Italian ricotta
  cheese

1 teaspoon chopped fresh
  thyme or parsley

salt and freshly milled pepper

50 g (2 oz) feta cheese

**Serves 4**

Preparation time: 20 minutes

Cooking time: 35 minutes

**1** Keep the filo pastry sheets stacked and cover with a damp cloth. Melt the butter and oil together for brushing the filo sheets. Brush a 25 cm (10 inch) fluted tart tin (with removable base) with a little of the melted butter.

**2** Take one filo sheet at a time and cut each in half. Brush the pastry piece with melted butter. Lay, buttered side up, over the base of the tin allowing the pastry to overhang the tart tin rim by about 5 cm (2 inches). Repeat the process with the remaining pastry sheets, and adjust the direction each time one is laid in the tart tin so that the corners fall like the petals of a flower. Turn the filo pastry edges into the tart in a crinkly fashion to make a pretty border.

**3** Halve the fresh dates and remove the stones. Slice the dates lengthways into slivers. Sprinkle half of the dates and half of the toasted pine kernels over the filo tart base.

**4** Heat the oven to 190°C (375°F or gas no. 5). Turn the eggs, cream and ricotta cheese into a mixing bowl and whisk together until thoroughly blended. Add the chopped herbs and season well with salt and freshly milled pepper. Cut the feta cheese into small cubes.

**5** Pour the mixture into the filo tart. Scatter the feta cheese cubes, remaining slivered dates and toasted pine kernels over the top. Set in the heated oven and bake for 30–35 minutes, until the filling has set and the pastry is golden brown and crisp. Serve warm.

# Cheese and Tomato Enchiladas

**1** Peel and finely chop the onion and peel and crush the garlic. Heat the oil in a medium saucepan, add the onion and allow to soften. Stir in the garlic.

**2** Add the mild chilli powder, cumin and oregano and stir for a moment over the heat. Add the tinned tomatoes and juice, the sugar, tomato purée and a seasoning of salt and pepper. Bring to a simmer and allow to cook gently, uncovered, for about 20 minutes or until reduced to a thick tomato chilli sauce. Draw off the heat.

**3** Heat the oven to 180°C (350°F or gas no. 4). Place the flour tortillas in a stack, wrap them in a foil parcel and warm them in the oven as it heats up. Grate the cheese. Open the parcel of warmed tortillas. Taking one tortilla at a time spread a spoonful of tomato chilli sauce and a sprinkling of grated cheese onto each. Tightly roll them up and place, seam down, in an ungreased 1.7 litre (3 pint) baking dish. Spread a little of the tomato chilli sauce over the first layer of rolled-up enchiladas before starting a second layer.

**4** Spoon over any remaining tomato chilli sauce and sprinkle with any remaining cheese. Set in the heated oven and bake for 20–25 minutes or until bubbling and hot. Serve with a bowl of soured cream to spoon over each serving of enchiladas. Pass round a salad of leafy greens and diced avocado.

1 large onion
2 cloves garlic
2 tablespoons olive oil
2 teaspoons mild chilli powder
1 teaspoon ground cumin
1 teaspoon dried oregano
2 x 400 g tins chopped tomatoes in juice
1 teaspoon caster sugar
1 tablespoon concentrated tomato purée
salt and freshly milled pepper
9 flour tortillas
250 g (9 oz) mature Cheddar cheese
soured cream and leafy green salad with diced avocado to serve

**Serves 3**
Preparation time: 40 minutes
Cooking time: 20–25 minutes

# Smoked Salmon with Warm Potato Salad

**1** Scrub the new potatoes, add to a pan of boiling salted water and simmer for 10 minutes or until knife-tip tender.

**2** Trim the spring onions, then chop all the white and some of the green stems. Measure the white wine vinegar, mustard and honey into a mixing bowl. Add a seasoning of salt and pepper, the olive oil and the chopped fresh dill. Mix with a fork to blend the dressing.

**3** Drain the potatoes and dry on a tea cloth. Slice the potatoes thickly and, while hot, turn into the dressing. Arrange the sliced smoked salmon on serving plates. Add a spoonful of warm potato salad and the delicious dressing.

450 g (1 lb) new potatoes
1 bunch (6–8) spring onions
2 tablespoons white wine vinegar
1 tablespoon Dijon mustard
1 tablespoon clear honey
salt and freshly milled pepper
75 ml (3 fl oz) olive oil
2 tablespoons chopped fresh dill
350 g (12 oz) smoked salmon

**Serves 4**
Preparation time: 15 minutes
Cooking time: 10 minutes

# Spinach and Prawn Filo Pastry Pie

1 x 350 g bag small leaf
  spinach
200 g (7 oz) feta cheese
225 g (8 oz) frozen peeled
  prawns, thawed
salt and freshly milled black
  pepper
8 sheets fresh filo pastry
50 g (2 oz) butter
2 tablespoons grapeseed oil
1–2 teaspoons toasted sesame
  seeds

**Serves 4**

Preparation time: 20 minutes
Cooking time: 40 minutes

**1** Turn the spinach leaves straight into a saucepan and sprinkle with a few drops of cold water. Set over a moderate heat and cover with the pan lid. Cook long enough for the leaves to wilt, about 2 minutes. Then drain the spinach in a colander and press well to extract all the water. Chop the spinach coarsely.

**2** Turn the spinach into a mixing bowl. Break the feta cheese into chunky pieces and add to the spinach along with the peeled prawns. Season well with salt and freshly milled pepper and stir gently to mix.

**3** Keep the filo pastry sheets stacked and covered with a damp cloth to make sure they don't become brittle. Heat the butter with the grapeseed oil. Brush a 20 cm (8 inch) fluted flan tin (with removable base) with melted butter and oil. Take 6 filo sheets one at a time and cut in half. Brush each piece with melted butter and oil. Lay the filo sheets (buttered side up) over the base of the tin, allowing the filo pastry edges to overhang by about 5 cm (2 inches), adjusting the direction each time one is laid in the tin, so that the corners fall like the petals of a flower.

**4** Turn the spinach filling into the filo-lined tin. Draw up the overhanging pastry from around the edges and turn in over the pie filling. Brush the last two sheets of filo with butter and oil. Crinkle the filo sheets and lay (buttered side up) over the pie to fill in the centre. Sprinkle the pie top generously with toasted sesame seeds.

**5** Heat the oven to 180°C (350°F or gas no. 4). Set the filo pie in the heated oven and bake for 40 minutes. About 10 minutes before the baking time is up, lift the pie from the flan tin (using the removable base). Return the pie to the oven to complete baking and crisp up the sides.

# Mild Vegetable Curry

**1** All the vegetables should be cut into attractive shapes: trim and thickly slice the courgettes, break the cauliflower into florets, trim the beans and cut into 2.5 cm (1 inch) pieces, scrub the new potatoes (leave the skins on) and cut in slices. Put all the vegetables together. Peel and finely chop the onion. Peel and crush the garlic.

**2** Heat the oil in a 25 cm (10 inch) frying pan or a flameproof casserole. Add the onion, sprinkle with the sugar and stir over a low heat to soften. Add the crushed garlic, stirring in well, then the tomato purée. Cook for a moment. Stir in the spices and give them a minute over the heat. Blend in the vegetable stock and then the single cream.

**3** Add all the prepared vegetables and turn them in the spicy liquid. Halve, core and slice in the apple. Drain the can of chickpeas, rinse and add to the mixture. Season with salt and freshly milled pepper and stir. Bring to the boil, lower the heat to a simmer, cover with the pan lid and cook gently for 30–40 minutes, or until the vegetables are tender.

**4** Meanwhile chop or crumble the coconut cream. Sprinkle over the vegetable curry and stir in, the spicy sauce should thicken evenly. Draw off the heat, sprinkle with the toasted sesame seeds and add a garnish of Fried Onion Rings.

**Fried Onion Rings:** Peel 1 medium onion, slice thinly and separate out the rings. Combine 1 tablespoon flour, ½ teaspoon ground cumin and ½ teaspoon ground coriander. Shake the onion rings in the flour mixture to coat, then shallow fry in 1 tablespoon olive oil until brown and crisp.

900 g (2 lb) mixed vegetables – courgettes, cauliflower, green beans and new potatoes, in any proportions you like

1 medium onion

2 cloves garlic

1 tablespoon olive oil

1 teaspoon caster sugar

1 tablespoon concentrated tomato purée

1 teaspoon ground turmeric

1 teaspoon ground coriander

½ teaspoon mild chilli powder

400 ml (¾ pint) vegetable stock

300 ml (½ pint) single cream

1 medium cooking apple

1 x 432 g tin chickpeas

salt and freshly milled pepper

50 g (2 oz) creamed coconut

1 tablespoon toasted sesame seeds

Fried Onion Rings to garnish (recipe left)

**Serves 3**
Preparation time: 40 minutes
Cooking time: 30–40 minutes

# Smoked and Fresh Salmon Mousse

1 piece fresh salmon, about
  550 g (1¼ lb)
15 g (½ oz) powdered gelatine
150 ml (¼ pint) mayonnaise
150 ml (¼ pint) natural whole
  milk yoghurt
1 teaspoon onion juice – see
  recipe
salt and freshly milled pepper
½ teaspoon paprika
oil for greasing
1 x 113 g packet smoked
  salmon (about 4 slices)
300 ml (½ pint) double cream
crisp lettuce leaves and Honey
  and Dill Dressing (recipe
  below) to serve

**Serves 6**

Preparation time: 30 minutes,
  plus cooling and chilling time
Cooking time: 1 minute

**1** Rinse the salmon piece and place in a saucepan. Add cold water to cover and then remove the salmon piece. Bring the water to the boil, replace the salmon in the saucepan and, when the water boils, boil for 1 minute only and draw off the heat. Cover with the pan lid and leave in a cool place overnight. The next day the salmon will be perfectly cooked and quite cold. Lift the salmon from the pan, remove the skin and bones and flake the flesh.

**2** Measure 75 ml (3 fl oz) cold water into a small saucepan and sprinkle in the gelatine. Let it stand for 5 minutes, then stir over a low heat until the gelatine has dissolved – do not boil. Measure the mayonnaise and yoghurt into a large bowl and stir to blend. Add the dissolved gelatine and mix through. Add the onion juice – grate the cut side of a peeled, halved onion on a fine grater and spoon up the juice – salt and pepper and the paprika. Stir and stand for about 30 minutes or until it starts to set

**3** Meanwhile, rub a drop or two of oil around the inside of a 1.7 litre (3 pint) ring mould. Separate the slices of smoked salmon and lay inside the mould, spacing them apart. Fold the flaked fresh salmon into the mayonnaise mixture. Whip the cream to soft peaks and fold into the salmon mixture. Pour into the lined mould and spread level. Cover and refrigerate until set. Unmould the mousse and decorate with crisp lettuce leaves. Serve with Honey and Dill Dressing.

**Honey and Dill Dressing:** In a bowl combine 2 tablespoons white wine vinegar, 1 tablespoon Dijon mustard, 1 tablespoon clear honey, a seasoning of salt and pepper and 75 ml (3 fl oz) olive oil. Stir well, then mix in 2 tablespoons chopped fresh dill.

# Spiced Rice with Smoked Salmon

*Use smoked salmon to garnish this sumptuous recipe – kedgeree like you've never had it before.*

**1** Add the saffron strands to the hot vegetable stock and infuse for 5 minutes. Peel and finely slice the onion. Rinse the basmati rice in cold water and drain well.

**2** Melt the butter in a 25 cm (10 inch) frying pan (with a lid), add the fennel and mustard seeds and heat, stirring until the mustard seeds begin to pop. Stir in the sliced onion, cover and cook gently for 5–6 minutes or until the onion is soft and translucent.

**3** Add the basmati rice. Stir and cook for 2 minutes. Add the saffron stock and bring to a simmer. Season with salt and pepper, cover and cook 15–20 minutes until the rice grains are tender and the stock has been absorbed.

**4** Meanwhile add the smoked haddock to a pan of simmering water and poach for 10 minutes. Then drain, skin and flake the flesh. Cut the smoked salmon into ribbons. Combine the cream and curry paste and heat gently.

**5** Fold the flaked smoked haddock into the spiced rice along with the smoked mussels. Pile the mixture on 4 heated plates. Top with the smoked salmon ribbons and spoon over the hot curry sauce.

pinch of saffron strands
600 ml (1 pint) vegetable stock
1 medium onion
225 g (8 oz) basmati rice
50 g (2 oz) butter
1 teaspoon fennel seeds
1 teaspoon yellow mustard seeds
salt and freshly milled pepper
450 g (1 lb) smoked haddock
225 g (8 oz) smoked salmon
300 ml (½ pint) double cream
1 teaspoon curry paste
225 g (8 oz) smoked mussels

**Serves 4**
Preparation time: 15 minutes
Cooking time: 30–35 minutes

---

## Katie's Tip

Saffron imparts a wonderful seasonal golden colour to recipes, use it in other ways too. If you start with a concentrated infusion by soaking a few strands of saffron in 1–2 tablespoons boiling water (no more) until the liquid is bright orange, you can stir the infusion into cooked and drained rice for a salad, into mayonnaise for a dressing or a cream sauce for chicken and shellfish and as it is absorbed you will see the saffron yellow colour coming up.

# Potato Pizza

900 g (2 lb) baking potatoes
salt and freshly milled pepper
50 g (2 oz) butter
2–3 tablespoons olive oil
450 g (1 lb) plum tomatoes
pinch of sugar
3–4 fresh thyme sprigs
1 x 150 g packet Italian
   mozzarella cheese

**Serves 4**
Preparation time: 15 minutes.
  plus chilling time
Cooking time: 30–35 minutes

**1** Scrub the potatoes, put them in a large pan of cold water and bring to the boil. Simmer for 10 minutes to partly cook, drain and allow to cool. Skin, then chill in the refrigerator for at least 1 hour.
**2** Coarsely grate the potatoes and season. Heat half the butter and 1 tablespoon of oil in a non-stick frying pan. Add the grated potato, spreading them evenly, and press down all over with a spatula to form a thick layer. Fry over a moderate heat for 15–20 minutes.
**3** When the potato layer is hot and the underside crisp and golden, cover with a plate, invert the pan and turn the potato layer onto it. Add the rest of the butter to the hot pan and slide the potato back. Fry, uncovered, for a further 5–10 minutes.
**4** Meanwhile, heat the grill until hot and set the grill rack 7.5 cm (3 inches) below the heat source. Slice the tomatoes in half and brush with olive oil. Season with salt and pepper and a pinch of sugar. Set under the heated grill for about 5 minutes or until the tomatoes are tender, but not soft.
**5** Arrange the tomatoes over the potato layer. Scatter with fresh thyme leaves and top with slices of mozzarella and a drizzle of olive oil. Slide the pan under the grill to melt the cheese. Serve in wedges.

# Baked Cheese Soufflé Potatoes

*You could tuck a surprise such as flaked smoked mackerel underneath the potato filling.*

**1** Heat the oven to 220°C (425°F or gas no. 7). Scrub the potatoes then prick them with a skewer. Set in the heated oven (spaced apart) and bake for 1 hour or until the potatoes feel soft. Remove the potatoes from the oven and lower the oven heat to 180°C (350°F or gas no. 4).

**2** With a sharp kitchen knife, slice each potato in half lengthways. Scoop the soft potato flesh into a mixing bowl. Arrange the potato shells on a baking tray and replace in the oven to crisp them up. Mash the potato with a fork. Mix in the grated cheese, a seasoning of salt and freshly milled pepper and a grating of nutmeg.

**3** Separate the eggs. Add the butter, cream and egg yolks to the potato mixture and beat with a wooden spoon until smooth and soft. Whisk the egg whites to stiff peaks and fold them into the potato mixture with a metal tablespoon. Pile the mixture back into the potato skins and then return to the oven for 20–25 minutes or until golden before serving.

4 medium potatoes for baking
100 g (4 oz) grated Gruyère
  cheese
salt and freshly milled pepper
grated nutmeg
2 eggs
100 g (4 oz) butter
4 tablespoons double cream

**Serves 4**

Preparation time: 15 minutes
Cooking time: 1–1½ hours

# Grilled Vegetables with Halloumi Cheese

**1** Quarter the peppers lengthways and remove the seeds. Trim, then slice the courgettes on the diagonal. Cut across the aubergine in 5 mm (¼ inch) thick slices. Peel the onion and cut into thick slices – do not separate the rings. Cut the halloumi into thick slices.

**2** Heat the grill until hot and set the grill rack about 7.5 cm (3 inches) below the heat source. Crowd the vegetables onto one or more baking trays and brush with olive oil.

**3** Place the vegetables under the heat and grill until softened and tinged with brown, turn them over, brush with olive oil and grill the other side. As the vegetables are cooked, transfer them to a platter. Add the thyme. Lastly, arrange slices of halloumi on the tray and grill until melting and soft. Lightly toast the pine kernels in a dry pan.

**4** Arrange an assortment of grilled vegetables on each hot plate. Top with grilled halloumi and sprinkle over the toasted pine kernels.

3 yellow sweet peppers
2 medium courgettes
1 large aubergine
1 medium onion
100 g (4 oz) halloumi cheese
4–6 tablespoons olive oil
2–3 fresh thyme sprigs
2 tablespoons pine kernels

**Serves 3**

Preparation time: 20 minutes
Cooking time: 10 minutes

# Smoked Mackerel and New Potato Salad in a Mustard Dressing

3 peppered smoked mackerel
  fillets
1 bunch (6–8) spring onions
450 g (1 lb) new potatoes
1 x 142 ml carton soured
  cream
2 tablespoons mayonnaise
1 teaspoon Dijon mustard
1 tablespoon grainy mustard
1 tablespoon white wine
  vinegar
salt and freshly milled pepper
crisp lettuce to serve
2 tablespoons chopped fresh
  chives

**Serves 4**

Preparation time: 15 minutes
Cooking time: 10–15 minutes

**1** Remove the skin from the peppered mackerel fillets, then flake the flesh into chunky pieces. Trim the spring onions, then chop all of the white and some of the green stems.

**2** Scrub the new potatoes, leaving the skins on. Add to boiling salted water and cook for 10–15 minutes until tender. Drain and turn onto a clean tea cloth to dry the surfaces. Cool, then slice the potatoes thickly.

**3** In a mixing bowl, combine the soured cream, mayonnaise, both mustards and the wine vinegar. Add a seasoning of salt and pepper. Add the potatoes and spring onions and toss to mix. Add the smoked mackerel and toss again.

**4** Turn the mackerel salad into a serving bowl lined with crisp lettuce leaves and sprinkle with the chopped chives.

# Pork Sausages with Puy Lentils

175 g (6 oz) Puy lentils
1 medium onion
2 cloves garlic
450 g (1 lb) pork sausages
1 tablespoon olive oil
15 g (½ oz) butter
75 g (3 oz) bacon lardons
1 teaspoon caster sugar
½ teaspoon herbes de Provence
  or dried thyme
175 ml (6 fl oz) vegetable stock
freshly milled pepper
2 tablespoons chopped fresh
  parsley

**Serves 3**

Preparation time: 40 minutes
Cooking time: 30 minutes

**1** Rinse the lentils, cover with cold water and cook according to the packet instructions for 20 minutes, then drain. Peel and finely slice the onion and peel and crush the garlic.

**2** Separate the sausages, but don't prick them. Heat the oil in a 25 cm (10 inch) frying pan (with a lid). Add the sausages and fry to brown them on all sides. Remove the sausages from the pan.

**3** Add the butter to the hot pan drippings, then add the sliced onion and bacon lardons. Sprinkle with the sugar, stir and fry the mixture until the onion is soft and beginning to brown and the bacon pieces are frizzled. Stir in the garlic, then the herbs.

**4** Add the drained lentils and return the sausages to the pan. Stir in the vegetable stock and season with freshly milled pepper. Cover with the pan lid and simmer gently for 20 minutes – the lentils will finish cooking and absorb the stock. Sprinkle with chopped parsley and serve with crusty bread and Dijon mustard.

# Hazelnut-Stuffed Mushrooms

**1** Remove stalks and peel the open mushrooms. Peel and finely chop the onion and peel and crush the garlic. Pare and finely grate the carrot. Finely chop the chestnut mushrooms.

**2** Heat the olive oil in a large 25 cm (10 inch) frying pan. Add the onion, garlic, carrot, soy sauce and chopped chestnut mushrooms. Stir and let the mixture soften over a low heat for 10 minutes.

**3** Heat the oven to 180°C (350°F or gas no. 4). Toast the skinned hazelnuts in the oven, then chop finely in a food processor. Place the breadcrumbs, parsley, hazelnuts, a seasoning of salt and pepper and grated nutmeg into a mixing bowl. Add the softened vegetable mixture and lightly mixed egg. Mix ingredients with a fork.

**4** Take tablespoonfuls of stuffing mixture and press onto each open mushroom. Arrange the filled mushrooms in a single layer on an oiled baking tray or in a roasting tin. Dust generously with paprika. Drizzle melted butter over the mushrooms. Bake for 20 minutes and serve hot.

8 large open mushrooms
1 medium onion
1 clove garlic
1 medium carrot
100 g (4 oz) chestnut mushrooms
2 tablespoons olive oil
1 tablespoon soy sauce
100 g (4 oz) skinned hazelnuts
50 g (2 oz) white breadcrumbs
2 tablespoons chopped fresh
  parsley
salt and freshly milled pepper
grated nutmeg
1 egg
paprika for dusting
50 g (2 oz) butter, melted

**Serves 3–4**
Preparation time: 25 minutes
Cooking time: 20 minutes

# Pasta

Pasta is for the spontaneous cook, assembled oven-baked dishes apart, it should be cooked and served straight away. Some of these recipes are so quick, you can easily get the additional ingredients ready while the pasta cooks. Pretty pasta shapes are charming and so much easier to eat with a fork. I like to mix the shapes, then toss and serve, perhaps with a side salad and some delicious bread.

*Pasta Shells with Ricotta and Spinach in Tomato Ragu*

# Pasta Shells with Ricotta and Spinach in Tomato Ragu

12 large pasta shells –
  conchiglie
225 g (8 oz) fresh spinach
225 g (8 oz) ricotta cheese
salt and freshly milled pepper
grated nutmeg
700 g (1½ lb) ripe tomatoes
2–3 cloves garlic
2 tablespoons olive oil
fresh thyme sprig
2 tablespoons grated
  Parmesan cheese

**Serves 4**
Preparation time: 30 minutes
Cooking time: 40 minutes

**1** Add the pasta shells to a saucepan of boiling salted water, stir as the water reboils and cook for 10 minutes until barely tender. Drain, then plunge the pasta shells into a bowl of cold water to cool them.
**2** Meanwhile, wash the spinach in cold water. Pull away the stalks, pile the leaves into a colander and blanch them by pouring through the contents of a kettle of boiling water. Drain and press the spinach well to extract the moisture, then chop coarsely.
**3** Turn the ricotta cheese into a mixing bowl. Season with salt, freshly milled pepper and a little grated nutmeg. Add the chopped spinach and mix. Stuff each pasta shell with spoonfuls of the ricotta and spinach mixture, then place the filled shells in an oiled 1.1 litre (2 pint) baking dish.
**4** Cut out and discard the stalk ends from the tomatoes, then cut the tomatoes coarsely – no need to remove the skins. Peel and crush the garlic. Warm the olive oil in a saucepan, add the garlic and heat for a moment, so the oil takes the flavour of the garlic. Add the tomatoes and the thyme and let the mixture simmer for 15–20 minutes or until a thick sauce has formed. Spoon the tomato sauce over the filled pasta shells. Up to this stage you can prepare the recipe in advance – refrigerate no longer than overnight.
**5** Heat the oven to 180°C (350°F or gas no. 4). Sprinkle the pasta shells with the grated Parmesan, then set them in the heated oven and bake for 15–20 minutes or until bubbling. Serve hot.

## Katie's Tip

The ideal state for cooked pasta is *al dente*, which means it has some bite to it and is not completely soft. But, for filled shells which are subsequently baked, shorten the cooking time by a few minutes to allow for additional cooking in the oven. If you drain the pasta shells then plunge them into cold water for a moment, they'll be easier to handle for filling.

# Roasted Red Pepper Cannelloni

**1** Halve, deseed and quarter the red peppers. Cut out and discard the stalk ends of the tomatoes and cut up the tomatoes coarsely. Peel and crush the garlic.

**2** Arrange the pepper pieces, skin side up, on a grill tray and brush with a little olive oil. Set under a heated grill until the skins have blackened. Turn the pepper pieces, brush with oil again and grill the other sides for a few minutes to soften them. Let the pepper pieces cool, peel of the skins and chop the peppers coarsely.

**3** Heat 1 tablespoon of the oil in a saucepan. Add the crushed garlic and sauté for a moment to flavour the oil. Add the chopped tomatoes and a seasoning of salt and pepper. Cook gently until the mixture has reduced to a thick purée – about 20 minutes. Spread 2 tablespoons of the tomato mixture over the base of an oiled 1.1 litre (2 pint) baking dish. Add the chopped sweet pepper to the remaining sauce and allow to cool. Spoon the roasted red pepper and tomato mixture into the cannelloni shells to fill them and set the shells in a single layer in the dish.

**4** Melt the butter in a saucepan, stir in the flour and cook for a moment. Then gradually stir in the milk, beating well all the time to make a smooth quite thin sauce. Season with salt and pepper and a grating of nutmeg. Stir in all but 1 tablespoon of the grated cheese. Pour over the cannelloni to cover. Sprinkle with remaining cheese. Up to this stage you can prepare the recipe ahead – refrigerate no longer than 24 hours.

**5** Preheat the oven to 180°C (350°F or gas no. 4). Set the dish of cannelloni in the oven and bake for 40 minutes until bubbling.

2 red sweet peppers
700 g (1½ lb) tomatoes
2 cloves garlic
1–2 tablespoons olive oil
salt and freshly milled pepper
12 quick-cooking cannelloni
  shells
25 g (1 oz) butter
25 g (1 oz) flour
400 ml (¾ pint) milk
grated nutmeg
50 g (2 oz) grated Parmesan
  cheese

**Serves 4**
Preparation time: 40 minutes
Cooking time: 1 hour

---

### Katie's Tip

Grilling brings out the natural sweet flavour of certain vegetables. Red and yellow peppers, slices of onion, courgettes or aubergines are the most popular. It's easier to brush and turn them if they are arranged on a baking tray – choose one with a turned up edge to contain the juices.

# Tomato, Mascarpone and Black Olive Pasta

900 g (2 lb) plum tomatoes

2 cloves garlic

2 tablespoons olive oil

salt and freshly milled pepper

1 teaspoon sun-dried tomato paste

225 g (8 oz) pasta – penne or rotelle

2 rounded tablespoons mascarpone cheese

1 tablespoon chopped fresh or ½ teaspoon dried oregano

6–8 pitted black olives

**Serves 3**

Preparation time: 10 minutes

Cooking time: 30 minutes

**1** Cut out and discard the stalk end of each tomato. Scald the tomatoes and peel away the skins. Chop the tomatoes coarsely. Peel and crush the garlic.

**2** Heat the olive oil in a medium saucepan. Add the garlic and fry for a moment to flavour the oil. Add all the tomatoes, a seasoning of salt and pepper and the sun-dried tomato paste. Cover with the pan lid and let the tomatoes stew for a few minutes to soften them. Then remove the lid and cook the sauce gently, stirring occasionally, until the tomato water has evaporated and you have a thick mixture – about 20 minutes.

**3** Meanwhile add the pasta to a saucepan of boiling salted water, stir as the water reboils and cook for 6–8 minutes until tender. Add the mascarpone to the tomato sauce and stir as it melts into the mixture. Add the oregano and olives.

**4** Drain the pasta and turn into a warmed serving bowl. Add the tomato, mascarpone and olive sauce and toss.

# Linguini with Pepper and Garlic Sauce

2 red sweet peppers

1 medium onion

2 cloves garlic

2 tablespoons olive oil

75 ml (3 fl oz) vegetable stock

4 tablespoons double cream

1 teaspoon red wine vinegar

salt and freshly milled pepper

1 tablespoon chopped fresh parsley

225 g (8 oz) linguini

grated Parmesan cheese to serve

**Serves 3**

Preparation time: 20 minutes

Cooking time: 15–20 minutes

**1** Heat the grill to hot and set the grill rack 7.5 cm (3 inches) from the heat source. Quarter the sweet peppers lengthways and discard the seeds. Arrange the pepper pieces (skin side up) on a baking tray and set under the grill until the skins are blistered and charred. Cover with a cloth and leave for 10 minutes by which time they should be cool enough to handle. Peel off the charred skins.

**2** Peel and finely slice the onion. Peel and crush the garlic. Gently fry the onion in the olive oil until softened. Add the garlic and stir. Add the pepper and stock, cover and cook gently for 6–8 minutes until softened.

**3** With a slotted spoon transfer the pepper pieces, onion and garlic to a food processor bowl and blend to a smooth purée. Add the stock from the pan, cream, wine vinegar and seasoning and blend again. Return the sauce to the pan and add the chopped parsley.

**4** Meanwhile add the linguini to a pan of boiling salted water, bring back to the boil, stirring and cook for 3–4 minutes, then drain. Reheat the sweet pepper sauce and combine with the hot freshly cooked pasta. Serve with grated cheese for sprinkling.

# Mixed Pasta with Smoked Mussels in Saffron Cream

**1** If you buy tinned smoked mussels drain them from the oil, or open a packet of vacuum-packed mussels. Put a pinch of saffron in a cup, add 1 tablespoon boiling water and let the saffron infuse for 5 minutes. The water will take the colour and flavour of the saffron. Peel and finely chop the shallots.

**2** Add the pasta to a saucepan of boiling salted water and stir as the water comes back to the boil. Heat the butter in a large 25 cm (10 inch) frying pan. Add the shallots and soften. Strain in the saffron infusion, add the cream and the mussels. Stir as the mixture comes to a simmer. Add the hot drained pasta and a good seasoning of salt and pepper. Toss lightly and serve.

100 g (4 oz) smoked mussels
good pinch of saffron strands
2 shallots
175 g (6 oz) mixed pasta
  shapes – fusilli and penne
25 g (1 oz) butter
150 ml (¼ pint) double cream
salt and freshly milled pepper

**Serves 2**
Preparation time: 15 minutes
Cooking time: 10 minutes

# Orecchiette with Tomatoes, Black Olives and Anchovy Crumbs

**1** Peel the onion, then slice across and separate the rings. Peel and crush the garlic. Rinse the tomatoes. Trim the crusts from the bread and grate into crumbs (or buzz in a food processor). Drain the oil from the anchovies into a frying pan. Cut the anchovies in half and separate out the fillets.

**2** Add the orecchiette to a saucepan of boiling salted water, stir as the water returns to the boil and simmer for 6–8 minutes until tender. Heat the anchovy oil, add the breadcrumbs and anchovy pieces and fry, stirring, until the crumbs are crisp and golden. Transfer to a plate.

**3** Add the olive oil to the frying pan. Add the onion rings and garlic and fry until softened. Stir in the cherry tomatoes. Add the vegetable stock and the vinegar and cook gently for a few minutes to soften the tomatoes.

**4** Add the hot drained pasta and a seasoning of freshly milled pepper. Turn to toss and heat the pasta, then serve. Top with the crunchy anchovy crumbs and black olives.

1 medium onion
2 cloves garlic
225 g (8 oz) cherry tomatoes
2 slices fresh white bread
1 x 50 g tin anchovies in oil
225 g (8 oz) orecchiette ('little ears')
2 tablespoons olive oil
150 ml (¼ pint) vegetable stock
1 tablespoon red wine vinegar
freshly milled pepper
50 g (2 oz) black olives

**Serves 2**
Preparation time: 15 minutes
Cooking time: 20 minutes

# Farfalle with Leaf Spinach, Garlic and Pecorino Cheese

**1** Coarsely chop the spinach. Peel and crush the garlic. Cut the Pecorino cheese into small dice. Add the farfalle to a saucepan of boiling salted water and stir as the water returns to the boil. Simmer for 6–8 minutes until tender.

**2** Heat the oil in a 25 cm (10 inch) frying pan and fry the garlic gently for 1–2 minutes – do not let the garlic brown. Add the spinach and stir-fry for 2 minutes. The leaves will reduce in volume. Remove from the heat, add the hot drained pasta, a seasoning of freshly milled pepper and the Pecorino cheese. Toss and serve.

1 x 200 g bag ready-prepared small leaf spinach
6 cloves garlic
75–100 g (3–4 oz) Pecorino cheese
225 g (8 oz) farfalle (bows)
3 tablespoons olive oil
freshly milled pepper

**Serves 2**
Preparation time: 10 minutes
Cooking time: 10–15 minutes

# Pasta Quills with Courgettes and Basil

300 g (11 oz) courgettes
1 medium onion
15 g (½ oz) (3–4 stalks) fresh
 basil or 2 tablespoons pesto
 sauce
225 g (8 oz) penne (quills)
50 g (2 oz) butter
1 tablespoon olive oil
salt and freshly milled pepper
3 tablespoons grated
 Parmesan cheese

**Serves 3**

Preparation time: 20 minutes
Cooking time: 10 minutes

**1** Rinse the courgettes, trim and discard the tops then grate the courgettes coarsely. Peel and finely chop the onion. Strip the basil leaves from their stems and chop them into shreds.

**2** Add the pasta to a saucepan of boiling salted water, stir as the water reboils and simmer for 6–8 minutes until tender.

**3** Meanwhile melt half the butter and the olive oil in a large 25 cm (10 inch) frying pan. Add the onion and cook gently until soft and a little golden. Add the courgettes and basil leaves (or pesto sauce) and stir-fry for 2–3 minutes until the courgettes have softened. Then season with salt and freshly milled pepper.

**4** Drain the pasta and turn into a warmed serving bowl. Add the remaining butter and the grated Parmesan and toss. Add the courgette mixture and toss again before serving.

# Campanelle with Oyster Mushrooms and Parmesan Cream

350 g (12 oz) oyster or brown
 cap mushrooms
3 cloves garlic
150 ml (¼ pint) double cream
salt and freshly milled pepper
2 tablespoons grated
 Parmesan cheese
225 g (8 oz) campanelle
 (trumpets)
50 g (2 oz) butter
2 tablespoons chopped fresh
 parsley

**Serves 3**

Preparation time: 15 minutes
Cooking time: 10 minutes

**1** Gently tear oyster mushrooms into large pieces or thickly slice brown cap mushrooms. Peel and crush the garlic. In a small bowl combine the cream, a seasoning of salt and pepper and half the grated Parmesan.

**2** Add the campanelle to a saucepan of boiling salted water and stir as the water returns to the boil. Simmer for 6–8 minutes until cooked. Meanwhile melt the butter in a large 25 cm (10 inch) frying pan. Add the garlic and stir for a moment, then add the mushrooms and parsley and sauté for 2–3 minutes until tender. Season with salt and pepper.

**3** Drain the pasta and return to the saucepan. Add the Parmesan cream and heat for a moment. Turn the pasta onto plates and top with the mushrooms, garlic and parsley. Serve with the remaining grated Parmesan sprinkled over.

# Fresh Tomato and Herb Pasta

**1** Cut out and discard stalk ends from the tomatoes. Scald tomatoes and peel away skins. Halve and scoop out the seeds, then coarsely chop the flesh. Place in a mixing bowl.

**2** Add the herbs – the parsley very finely chopped, the chives scissor-snipped and the basil leaves stripped from the stem and coarsely chopped. Season with salt and pepper and the sugar. Toss to mix.

**3** Add the pasta to a saucepan of boiling salted water, stir as the water reboils and cook for 6–8 minutes until tender, then drain. Warm the olive oil until hot. Add the hot pasta and hot olive oil to the tomatoes and toss the ingredients. Add the olives and toss again. Turn onto a serving platter. Serve with warmed olive ciabatta.

700 g (1½ lb) ripe tomatoes
2 tablespoons chopped fresh
 parsley
2 tablespoons snipped fresh
 chives
5–6 fresh basil sprigs
salt and freshly milled pepper
1 teaspoon caster sugar
225 g (8 oz) pasta – fusilli and
 penne
100 ml (4 fl oz) olive oil
6–8 pitted black olives

**Serves 3**
Preparation time: 15 minutes
Cooking time: 6–8 minutes

# Tagliatelle with Grilled Vegetables

**1** Halve, deseed and cut the peppers lengthways – each into about six pieces. Slice the aubergine in 1 cm (½ inch) thick slices. Peel the onion, cut in slices and separate into rings. Peel and slice the garlic.
**2** Crowd the pepper pieces on a baking tray (skin side up) and brush with a little olive oil. Grill until they soften and the skins scorch. Remove from the heat. Arrange the aubergine slices on the baking tray, brush with a little olive oil and grill until browned. Turn slices over to brown the other sides. Cut the sun-dried tomatoes in half.
**3** Add the tagliatelle to a saucepan of boiling salted water, and stir as the water comes back to the boil and simmer for 4–6 minutes until tender. Heat the remaining olive oil in a frying pan. Add the onion rings and fry to soften. Add the crushed garlic and stir, then add the grilled peppers, aubergine and sun-dried tomatoes. Add the stock, wine vinegar and a seasoning of salt and pepper. Bring to a simmer and cook gently for 5 minutes to soften the vegetables. Drain the pasta, turn into a serving bowl and toss with oil from the jar of sun-dried tomatoes. Serve the grilled vegetable mixture separately to spoon over the hot pasta.

3 sweet peppers – red, yellow and orange
1 medium aubergine
1 large onion
2 cloves garlic
4 tablespoons olive oil
12 sun-dried tomatoes in oil
225 g (8 oz) tagliatelle
150 ml (¼ pint) vegetable stock
2 tablespoons white wine vinegar
salt and freshly milled pepper
2 tablespoons oil from the jar of sun-dried tomatoes

**Serves 3**
Preparation time: 20 minutes
Cooking time: 15 minutes

# Pappardelle with Lamb Brochettes

**1** Trim, then cut the lamb fillet into bite-sized pieces. Crush the cloves garlic and remove the papery coating. Place the meat in a shallow dish. Add 3 tablespoons olive oil, the crushed garlic and the thyme leaves. Leave to marinate for about 4 hours, then spear the meat pieces onto 6 wooden skewers. Coarsely chop the sun-dried tomatoes.
**2** Heat the grill to hot and place the grill pan 7.5 cm (3 inches) below the heat source. Set the lamb brochettes under the heat and grill for 10–12 minutes, turning them occasionally. Meanwhile add the pappardelle to a saucepan of boiling salted water. Stir as the water reboils, then cook for 6 minutes, and drain.
**3** Turn the pasta into a mixing bowl, add the sun-dried tomato oil, the remaining olive oil and a good seasoning of salt and pepper and toss to mix.
**4** Fork the pappardelle and tomato mixture onto a serving platter. Arrange the lamb brochettes on top and squeeze lemon juice over the lamb.

225–275 g (8–10 oz) lamb neck fillet
2–3 cloves garlic
4 tablespoons olive oil
1 tablespoon fresh thyme leaves
75 g (3 oz) sun-dried tomatoes in oil
175 g (6 oz) pappardelle (wide noodle) pasta
2 tablespoons oil from the jar of sun-dried tomatoes
salt and freshly milled pepper
juice ½ lemon

**Serves 3**
Preparation time: 15 minutes, plus marinating time
Cooking time: 12–15 minutes

# Poultry and Game

Most chicken and turkey cuts can be pan-fried or grilled for quick cooking, rub them in delicious spices or add simple sauces and serve them straight away. Slow simmered sautés of chicken, rabbit and pheasant or succulent duck cooked with fruits are a good choice for entertaining. Take your pick.

*Chicken Provençal*

# Chicken Provençal

1 medium onion
2 cloves garlic
1 red sweet pepper
2 tablespoons olive oil
4 chicken drumsticks and
  4 thighs
25 g (1 oz) butter
75 ml (3 fl oz) dry white
  vermouth or dry white wine
1 x 400 g tin chopped
  tomatoes
2 sprigs fresh thyme
salt and freshly milled pepper
1 tablespoon concentrated
  tomato purée
1 tablespoon cornflour
6–8 black olives

**Serves 4**
Preparation time: 40 minutes
Cooking time: 40 minutes

**1** Peel and finely chop the onion and peel and crush the garlic. Halve, deseed and quarter the red pepper. Heat the grill to hot and set the grill rack at least 7.5 cm (3 inches) from the heat source. Crowd the red pepper pieces (skin side up) on a baking tray. Brush with 1 tablespoon of the olive oil. Set under the heat and grill until the skin is scorched and the peppers are softened.

**2** Heat the remaining olive oil in a large 25 cm (10 inch) frying pan. Add the chicken pieces and fry to brown them on all sides. Transfer the chicken from the pan to a casserole. Add the grilled pepper pieces tucking them in among the chicken.

**3** Pour off the excess pan drippings. Add the butter to the frying pan along with the chopped onion and fry gently to soften the onion. Stir in the garlic. Add the vermouth or white wine and stir to pick up all the flavouring. Pour the wine, onion and garlic into the casserole.

**4** Heat the oven to 180°C (350°F or gas no. 4). Press the contents of the tin of tomatoes through a sieve into a mixing bowl. Add the thyme, a seasoning of salt and pepper and the concentrated tomato purée. Blend the cornflour with 2 tablespoons cold water until smooth. Stir the cornflour blend into the tomato mixture. Pour the tomato mixture over the chicken pieces in the casserole. Cover with the casserole lid.

**5** Set the casserole in the heated oven and cook for 40 minutes. Stir and add black olives before serving.

### Katie's Tip
I often use dry white vermouth instead of wine in casseroles, for poaching fish or for adding to a risotto; it has a subtle herby flavour to it. If you're short of white wine for cooking purposes, try a dry cider which is very nice too.

# Chicken Cooked with Summer Peas

**1** Heat the oven to 160°C (325°F or gas no. 3). Trim the chicken pieces and season them with salt and freshly milled pepper. Peel the small onions leaving them whole, then blanch in boiling water for 5 minutes and drain.

**2** Melt 25 g (1 oz) of the butter in a large 25 cm (10 inch) frying pan. Add the chicken pieces and brown them on all sides. Transfer the chicken to a casserole. Pour off excess pan drippings. Add the onions and bacon lardons to the pan and fry until lightly coloured. Add to the chicken pieces.

**3** Deglaze the frying pan with the vegetable stock. Add the green peas. Remove the outer coarse leaves and shred the lettuce. Add the lettuce, remaining butter, the sugar and a seasoning of salt and freshly milled pepper. Combine the cornflour with 2 tablespoons cold water and stir in. Bring to the boil.

**4** Pour the contents of the pan over the chicken. Cover with the casserole lid, set in the heated oven and cook for 40 minutes.

4 cornfed chicken portions
salt and freshly milled pepper
8 small button onions
50 g (2 oz) butter
100 g (4 oz) bacon lardons
150 ml (5 fl oz) vegetable
   stock
250 g (9 oz) shelled peas
1 little gem lettuce
1 teaspoon caster sugar
1 tablespoon cornflour

**Serves 4**
Preparation time: 40 minutes
Cooking time: 40 minutes

# Chicken in a Mustard and Crème Fraîche Sauce

**1** Cut each chicken breast fillet into about 4 chunky pieces. Peel and crush the garlic. Strip the tarragon leaves from their stems and coarsely chop sufficient to make 2 good tablespoons.

**2** Heat the butter and oil in a large 25 cm (10 inch) frying pan (with a lid), add the chicken pieces and turn to seal and brown them – about 5 minutes.

**3** Add the crushed garlic and stir for a moment. Pour in the white wine and add the chopped tarragon. Bring to a simmer, cover with the pan lid and cook gently for about 10–15 minutes or until the chicken is tender.

**4** Remove the pan lid. Stir in the mustard, crème fraîche and a seasoning of salt and freshly milled pepper. Bring back to the boil, stirring. Serve.

4 skinless chicken breast fillets
2 cloves garlic
4–6 fresh tarragon sprigs
25 g (1 oz) butter
1 tablespoon olive oil
75 ml (3 fl oz) dry white wine
2 tablespoons Dijon mustard
1 x 200 g tub crème fraîche
salt and freshly milled pepper

**Serves 4**
Preparation time: 10 minutes
Cooking time: 30 minutes

# Chicken in a Lemon Tarragon Dressing

6 chicken breasts, with skin on
1 teaspoon olive oil
100–175 ml (4–6 fl oz)
  vegetable stock

FOR THE DRESSING:
rind and juice 1 lemon
1 tablespoon white wine
  vinegar
1 clove garlic
1 teaspoon Dijon mustard
2 teaspoons caster sugar
salt and freshly milled pepper
100 ml (4 fl oz) olive oil
4 tablespoons snipped fresh
  tarragon leaves
6–8 green olives to garnish

**Serves 8**
Preparation time: 50 minutes,
  plus cooling and marinating
Cooking time: 30–35 minutes

**1** Heat the oven to 180°C (350°F or gas no. 4). Arrange the chicken breasts, skin side up, in a deep baking dish or roasting tin, selecting one the right size to keep them closely packed. Brush the skins with a little olive oil. Pour in enough stock to come part way over the breasts, but not completely submerge them. Set in the oven, uncovered, and bake for 30–35 minutes. Let the breasts cool in the stock, then refrigerate (in the stock) until needed.

**2** For the dressing, combine the finely grated lemon rind, lemon juice and vinegar. Add the peeled and crushed garlic, mustard, sugar, salt and milled pepper and olive oil; mix well. Add the tarragon leaves.

**3** Lift the chicken breasts from the stock and pull away the skins. Slice the meat diagonally, or use a fork to tear it into strips. Arrange the chicken in one layer on a shallow serving dish. Spoon over the dressing, add the green olives to garnish and serve.

# Chicken in Crunchy Parmesan Crumbs

**1** Trim the fillets and cut each one lengthways and crossways into 4–5 chunky pieces. Combine the breadcrumbs, grated Parmesan, oregano, salt and a good seasoning of freshly milled pepper. Mix and spread the seasoned crumbs on a plate.

**2** Warm the butter with the olive oil in a saucepan and draw off the heat. Dip each chicken piece first in the warm butter, then in the seasoned crumbs to coat all over. Pat the crumb coating on firmly. Arrange the coated chicken pieces on a plate (or tray) and chill for at least 30 minutes or until ready to cook. In a bowl, combine the soured cream, mayonnaise and seasoning to taste, then chill.

**3** Heat the oven to 180°C (350°F or gas no. 4). Arrange the chicken pieces so that they are not touching, on one or more greased baking trays. Set in the preheated oven and bake for 20–25 minutes. Serve the chicken pieces hot with the chilled soured cream dip.

3 skinless chicken breast fillets

75 g (3 oz) fresh white or wholemeal breadcrumbs

25 g (1 oz) grated Parmesan cheese

1 tablespoon dried oregano

1 teaspoon salt

freshly milled pepper

25 g (1 oz) butter

1 tablespoon olive oil

FOR THE DIP:

1 x 142 ml carton soured cream

1 rounded tablespoon mayonnaise

salt and freshly milled pepper

**Serves 4**

Preparation time: 20 minutes, plus chilling time

Cooking time: 20–25 minutes

# Cajun-Spiced Chicken Spatchcock

*This American seasoning has a bite to it so it should be used sparingly; any left over could be rubbed over a roast chicken.*

2 poussins, about 400 g
  (14 oz) each
3 tablespoons olive oil
700 g (1½ lb) new potatoes
1 head garlic
freshly milled pepper

**FOR THE CAJUN SEASONING:**

2 tablespoons paprika
1 tablespoon coarse-ground
  black pepper
2 tablespoons dried oregano
1 tablespoon dried thyme
1 tablespoon dried onion
  flakes
½ teaspoon salt
½ teaspoon cayenne

**Serves 4**
Preparation time: 40 minutes
Cooking time: 35–40 minutes

**1** Split each poussin by cutting along both sides of the backbone with kitchen scissors. Remove the bone and flatten out each bird – turn the wing tips underneath and turn the thigh joints in towards the body. Skewer each bird with two satay sticks, pushing them crossways through the body to hold the shape. Rub the birds all over with 1 tablespoon of the olive oil.

**2** Combine all the ingredients for the Cajun seasoning in a bowl. Rub the seasoning over both sides of each bird; any remaining seasoning can be stored in a screw-topped jar.

**3** Heat the oven to 190°C (375°F or gas no. 5). Scrub the new potatoes but do not peel them. Slice the potatoes thickly, then add to a saucepan of boiling salted water along with the unpeeled head of garlic and blanch for 2 minutes, then drain. Reserve the head of garlic, then return the potatoes to the saucepan and shake them dry for a moment over the heat. Add the remaining 2 tablespoons of olive oil and toss the potatoes to coat them. Turn the potatoes into a roasting tin, season them with freshly milled pepper and add the whole head of garlic.

**4** Place a rack over the potatoes and arrange the poussins (skin side up) on the rack. Set in the heated oven and bake for 35–40 minutes or until the poussin juices run clear. Remove the satay sticks, then cut each poussin in half through the breastbone.

**5** Serve the poussins with the potatoes scooped from the roasting tin and the garlic – when the softened cloves are lightly pressed with a knife blade they will release a soft garlic purée.

# Crispy Grilled Lemon Chicken

**1** Trim the chicken breast fillets but leave the skin attached. Arrange them in one layer in a shallow dish. Grate the rind from one lemon onto a saucer, cover and set aside.

**2** Squeeze the juice from both lemons and pour over the chicken pieces. Cover and refrigerate overnight. Drain the chicken pieces from the lemon juice and pat dry with absorbent kitchen paper. Discard the lemon juice.

**3** Heat the oil in a frying pan. Add the chicken pieces and brown on both sides. Transfer to a baking dish, arranging them skin side up and closely packed together.

**4** Heat the oven to 180°C (350°F or gas no. 4). Sprinkle the reserved lemon rind over the chicken pieces. Add the chicken stock and tuck in the mint sprigs. Set in the heated oven and cook uncovered for 30 minutes. Let the chicken cool in the stock until it is serving time.

**5** Drain the chicken pieces and place skin side up on the grill rack. Sprinkle with the sugar and grill until golden and crisp. Serve warm with a lemon-flavoured mayonnaise.

4 chicken breast fillets, with
  skin on
2 lemons
2 tablespoons olive oil
225 ml (8 fl oz) chicken stock
2 fresh mint sprigs
1 tablespoon soft brown sugar

## Serves 4

Preparation time: 30 minutes,
  plus marinating time
Cooking time: 45 minutes

# Chicken with Mini Carrots in Boursin Sauce

**1** Cut each chicken breast into 4 chunky pieces. Wash and trim the mini carrots, but leave whole. Melt the butter in a large 25 cm (10 inch) frying pan (with a lid), add the chicken and gently brown all over. Add the carrots and stock. Bring to a simmer. Cover and cook gently for 10 minutes.

**2** When the chicken pieces are tender, add the Boursin cheese in pieces. Stir and turn the carrots and chicken as the cheese melts to form a sauce. Heat for a moment, then season with pepper. Sprinkle with chopped parsley and serve.

2 skinless chicken breast fillets
175 g (6 oz) mini carrots
25 g (1 oz) butter
50 ml (2 fl oz) chicken stock
1 x 80 g Boursin cheese,
  flavoured with garlic and
  herbs
freshly milled pepper
chopped fresh parsley to serve

## Serves 2

Preparation time: 10 minutes
Cooking time: 15 minutes

# Turkey Sauté with Browned Onions and Cranberry Sauce

**1** Cut the turkey meat into chunky pieces. Peel the onions leaving them whole.

**2** Heat the olive oil in a 25 cm (10 inch) frying pan (with a lid), add the turkey pieces and fry to seal and lightly colour them – about 5 minutes. Remove from the pan.

**3** Add the onions or shallots to the hot oil and fry, shaking the pan so that the onions roll over and brown quickly. Add the sherry and let the mixture bubble up. Add the cranberry sauce, the vegetable stock and balsamic vinegar. Bring to a simmer, stirring to dissolve the cranberry sauce.

**4** Return the turkey pieces to the pan. Cover with the pan lid and simmer for 20 minutes. Serve with the browned onions and sauce from the pan.

700 g (1½ lb) large turkey
    breast fillets
8 whole baby onions or
    shallots
2 tablespoons olive oil
2 tablespoons dry sherry
1 x 190 g jar cranberry sauce
175 ml (6 fl oz) vegetable
    stock
1 tablespoon balsamic vinegar

**Serves 4**

Preparation time: 15 minutes
Cooking time: 25 minutes

# Rolled Chicken in Parma Ham

**1** Flatten each chicken breast by beating with a rolling pin and season with salt and freshly milled pepper. Trim the mushrooms and chop finely, then, using a fork, mash with the garlic butter. Spread each chicken breast with the mushroom mixture and roll up. Overwrap with a slice of Parma ham and fix with a cocktail stick. Refrigerate until ready to cook.

**2** Heat the oil in a large 25 cm (10 inch) frying pan (with a lid), add the rolled chicken pieces and fry, turning to seal them on all sides. Add the chicken stock, bring to a simmer, cover with the pan lid and cook gently for 30 minutes.

**3** When the chicken is tender, remove the pan lid and discard the cocktail sticks. Top each chicken roll with a slice of cheese. Set under a heated grill until the cheese is bubbling and serve.

4 skinless chicken breast fillets
salt and freshly milled pepper
100 g (4 oz) chestnut
    mushrooms
50 g (2 oz) garlic butter
4 slices Parma ham
1 tablespoon olive oil
75 ml (3 fl oz) chicken stock
4 thin slices Emmental or
    Gruyère cheese

**Serves 4**

Preparation time: 20 minutes,
    plus chilling time
Cooking time: 35–40 minutes

# Cold Duck with Sweet and Sour Onions and Raisins

350 g (12 oz) button onions

100 ml (4 fl oz) red wine vinegar

25 g (1 oz) soft brown sugar

3 tablespoons olive oil

1 tablespoon concentrated
  tomato purée

salt and freshly milled pepper

2 bay leaves

3 fresh thyme sprigs

25 g (1 oz) seedless raisins

2 Barbary duck breasts

**Serves 6**

Preparation time: 25 minutes,
  plus cooling time

Cooking time: 1¾ hours

**1** Heat the oven to 140°C (275°F or gas no. 1). Top and tail the onions, pour boiling water over them and leave for 5 minutes, then drain. Slip off the skins and put onions in a casserole.

**2** Add the red wine vinegar, 150 ml (¼ pint) water, the sugar, olive oil, tomato purée and a seasoning of salt and pepper. Add the bay leaves, thyme sprigs and seedless raisins. Cover with the casserole lid. Set in the heated oven and cook for 1¼ hours until the onions are tender and in a delicious syrup. Allow to cool.

**3** Raise the oven temperature to 200°C (400°F or gas no. 6). Prick the skin on each duck fillet and rub the skins with salt. Set the duck fillets, skin side up, on a rack in a roasting tin. Set the duck in the heated oven and roast for 30–35 minutes – nicest if the duck is still a little pink. Allow the duck fillets to cool.

**4** With a sharp carving knife, slice the duck breasts thinly across the grain. Arrange the slices in a serving dish, spoon over the onions, raisins and dressing to serve.

---

## SOMETHING TO MULL OVER

• Measure 175 g (6 oz) caster sugar and 300 ml (½ pint) water into a large stainless steel saucepan (aluminium will taint the mull). Stir over a low heat to dissolve the sugar.

• Add 3–4 cloves and a piece of stick cinnamon. Bring to the boil, draw off the heat and infuse for 10 minutes. Extract the cloves and the cinnamon.

• Slice 2 oranges thinly. Add to the pan along with 2 bottles of red wine and 50 ml (2 fl oz) Cointreau. Heat slowly until the mull is pleasantly warmed (do not boil) and draw off the heat.

• Peel 1 lemon, taking off rind and white pith, then slice the fruit and add.

• Transfer to a punch bowl and serve. Makes 15 glasses.

# Roast Pheasant with Oatmeal Stuffing

4 streaky bacon rashers

2 oven-ready pheasants

15 g (½ oz) butter

1 large onion

flour for dusting

175 ml (6 fl oz) red wine

2 tablespoons rowan or
redcurrant jelly

FOR THE OATMEAL
STUFFING:

1 small onion

175 g (6 oz) medium oatmeal

75 g (3 oz) shredded beef suet

salt and freshly milled pepper

**Serves 4–6**

Preparation time: 30 minutes

Cooking time: 50 minutes–1 hour

**1** For the stuffing, peel and finely chop the onion. Put the oatmeal in a bowl. Add the suet, onion and seasoning. Sprinkle with 1–2 tablespoons water and mix – the stuffing will cling in small clumps.

**2** Heat the oven to 200°C (400°F or gas no. 6). Tie 2 streaky bacon rashers over each pheasant to baste the flesh. Spoon the stuffing into the body cavities – do not pack as the mixture will swell.

**3** Generously butter a roasting pan big enough to hold both birds without touching each other. Peel and thinly slice the onion and arrange in an even layer in the tin. Place the birds on top, breasts down. Set in the preheated oven and roast for 20 minutes.

**4** Turn the birds right side up, lift off the bacon and discard. Sprinkle the breasts lightly with flour (this helps them brown), baste with the pan drippings and return to the oven for a further 30 minutes. Transfer the pheasants to a warmed platter and keep hot.

**5** Set the roasting pan over a moderate heat to make the gravy. Add the wine and bring to the boil stirring to lift up any flavouring bits on the bottom of the pan. Stir in the jelly and continue to bubble until the jelly has melted. Strain the gravy into a warmed jug. Spoon the stuffing from the body cavity and serve with the sliced pheasant.

# Pheasant in Cream with Oyster Mushrooms

2 oven-ready pheasants

225 g (8 oz) oyster or
chestnut mushrooms

50 g (2 oz) butter

salt and freshly milled pepper

grated nutmeg

75 ml (3 fl oz) white
vermouth

200 ml (7 fl oz) double cream

1 large onion

**Serves 4**

Preparation time: 30 minutes

Cooking time: 1½ hours

**1** Heat the oven to 160°C (325°F or gas no. 3). Loosen any trussing around the pheasant. Cut chestnut mushrooms in thick slices; leave oyster mushrooms whole. Melt 25 g (1 oz) of the butter in a frying pan. Add the birds and brown all over. Remove to a plate.

**2** Add the remaining butter to the pan, add the mushrooms and sauté until the mushrooms soften and the juices run. Draw off the heat, season and add a grating of nutmeg. Spoon the mushrooms into the body cavity of each pheasant and place birds in a casserole.

**3** Replace the pan over the heat. Add the vermouth and stir. Bring to a simmer and boil rapidly for a few minutes to reduce and concentrate the flavour. Stir in the cream and draw off the heat. Peel and halve the onion, then finely slice and distribute around the pheasants in the casserole. Pour over the sauce from the frying pan.

**4** Cover and place the casserole in the oven and cook for 1½ hours. Split the pheasants in half to make 4 portions and return to the casserole. Keep hot until ready to serve.

# Pheasant Pâté

**1** Heat the oven to 160°C (325°F or gas no. 3). Place pheasants in a casserole large enough to take them both. Peel and slice 1 onion and add to the casserole along with 150 ml (¼ pint) water. Cover, set in the heated oven and cook for 1–1¼ hours until the pheasants are tender. Allow to cool. Thaw the chicken livers if they are frozen.

**2** Lift out the pheasants and take the meat off each carcass discarding skin and bones – use breast meat and tender pieces from the thighs only. Strain the stock and take the fat off the surface – if the birds have been chilled overnight, you will be able to lift off the solidified fat and the stock will be jellied. Reserve the stock.

**3** Pick over the chicken livers and separate them – include the pheasant livers if you have them. Peel and finely chop the remaining onion. Melt 50 g (2 oz) of the butter in a large 25 cm (10 inch) frying pan, add the chopped onion and fry gently to soften. Add the chicken livers, stir and turn them and cook for about 5 minutes until they are sealed and there is no sign of blood.

**4** Put the pheasant meat in a food processor bowl and buzz to chop finely. Add the contents of the frying pan, a good seasoning of salt and freshly milled pepper and the allspice. Add all the stock. Cover and buzz to a purée. Taste for seasoning.

**5** Spoon the pâté into a serving bowl and spread level. If the mixture is still warm, refrigerate until cold. Melt the remaining butter and pour over the top of the pâté to seal it. Sprinkle with chopped thyme leaves. Chill for several hours to firm up the mixture. Serve with toast or crusty bread or use it to fill sandwiches. The pâté will keep for 2–3 days.

2 oven-ready pheasants
2 medium onions
225 g (8 oz) chicken livers
90 g (3½ oz) butter
salt and freshly milled pepper
½ teaspoon ground allspice
chopped fresh thyme leaves
   to garnish

## Serves 6–8
Preparation time: 40 minutes,
   plus chilling time
Cooking time: 1–1½ hours

## Katie's Tip
Melted butter poured over the surface of a pâté seals it in the dish and helps to keep it moist; don't overheat the butter, if the butter is too hot when you pour it over it will tend to penetrate the mixture rather than form a surface layer. Add any garnish before the butter sets.

# Duck Cassoulet

*A cassoulet takes time to prepare but needs only reheating to serve.*

100 g (4 oz) streaky bacon
  rashers
4 duck breasts
4–6 venison or beef sausages
1 medium onion
3 stalks celery
2–3 cloves garlic
2 tablespoons olive oil
sprinkling of caster sugar
150 ml (¼ pint) red wine
1 tablespoon concentrated
  tomato purée
400 ml (¾ pint) vegetable
  stock
1 x 432 g tin green lentils
1 x 432 g tin cannellini beans

FOR THE TOPPING:

2–3 thick slices country bread
2 tablespoons grainy mustard
1 tablespoon olive oil

**Serves 4–6**

Preparation time: 40 minutes
Cooking time: 1–1½ hours

**1** Trim the bacon rashers and snip them into pieces. In a large 25 cm (10 inch) frying pan sauté the bacon pieces gently to crisp them. Transfer the bacon to a 1.1 litre (2 pint) casserole. Add the duck breasts to the hot frying pan (skin side down) and sauté to brown both sides. Transfer the duck breasts to the casserole. Add the sausages and sauté to colour them. Transfer to the casserole.

**2** Heat the oven to 180°C (350°F or gas no. 4). Peel and finely chop the onion. Trim and chop the celery and peel and crush the garlic. Add the oil to the frying pan. Add the onion and celery, sprinkle with the sugar and sauté gently to soften and brown – about 10 minutes. Stir in the garlic. With a perforated spoon transfer the vegetables to the casserole.

**3** Add the wine and tomato purée to the hot pan and stir. Bring to the boil, then pour over the contents of the casserole, along with the vegetable stock. Cover, set in the heated oven and cook for 30–40 minutes or until the duck is tender. Remove from the heat.

**4** Take out the duck breasts and slice each into 3 pieces on a slant, then put them back in the casserole. Drain and rinse the tins of lentils and cannellini beans, add them to the casserole and replace in the oven until bubbling hot.

**5** Cut the bread slices into chunky pieces. Combine the mustard and oil and spread this mixture on one side of each bread piece. Remove casserole lid and set bread pieces, mustard side up, on top of the duck, lentils and beans. Replace and bake until crunchy and brown – about 12–15 minutes.

# Braised Pheasant with Celery and Chestnuts

**1** Heat the oven to 160°C (325°F or gas no. 3). Joint the pheasants (see below). Peel the onions leaving them whole. Cut the celery stalks lengthways and across into sticks.

**2** Melt the butter and oil in a large 25 cm (10 inch) frying pan. Add all the onions and the pheasant pieces a few at a time. Turn the pheasant to seal and brown. Transfer the pheasant to a casserole and as the onions brown add them alongside.

**3** Add the celery to the hot pan drippings and sprinkle with the thyme, turn and cook for a few minutes. Add the celery to the casserole. Combine the stock, wine and tomato purée and add to the frying pan. Stir up any flavouring bits and bring to the boil. Pour over contents of the casserole. Add the bay leaves. Cover with the casserole lid. Set in the heated oven and cook for 50 minutes to 1 hour or until the pheasant is tender.

**4** Mix together the cornflour, 2 tablespoons cold water and the red wine vinegar. Stir into the contents of the casserole, add the chestnuts. Return to the oven for a further 15–20 minutes. Sprinkle with chopped parsley before serving.

**To joint a pheasant:** Start by using a knife to cut the skin between the leg and the breast, twist to dislocate the joint and cut the leg off. Repeat with the second leg. Set the bird back down. Slit along the breastbone to loosen the meat, then, starting from the cavity end cut the bird open with game shears or a knife. Open the bird out flat. Cut either side of the backbone and discard it. Then snip round and remove the rib cage. You now have 4 pieces. For 8 smaller pieces cut the legs in half through the joint and the breasts in half diagonally.

2 oven-ready pheasant
8 small onions
3–4 stalks celery
25 g (1 oz) butter
1 tablespoon olive oil
few leaves fresh or 1 teaspoon dried thyme
300 ml (½ pint) vegetable stock
300 ml (½ pint) red wine
1 tablespoon concentrated tomato purée
2 bay leaves
1 tablespoon cornflour
1 tablespoon red wine vinegar
1 x 200 g packet vacuum-packed, peeled and cooked chestnuts
1 tablespoon chopped fresh parsley

**Serves 4**
Preparation time: 25–30 minutes
Cooking time: 1½ hours

# Honey Glazed Duck with Grapefruit and Ginger Sauce

4 duck breast fillets

1 tablespoon clear honey

1 tablespoon dark soy sauce

FOR THE SAUCE:

3 grapefruits

50 g (2 oz) granulated sugar

300 ml (½ pint) unsweetened
  grapefruit juice

2 tablespoons clear honey

1 tablespoon dark soy sauce

juice 1 lemon

1 teaspoon grated fresh ginger

1 tablespoon cornflour

**Serves 6**

Preparation time: 35 minutes

Cooking time: 30–35 minutes

**1** Prick the skin on each duck fillet with a fork. Blend the honey and soy sauce to make a glaze and brush all over the duck. Set the duck fillets skin side up on a rack in a baking dish or roasting tin. Refrigerate while preparing the sauce.

**2** Slice away the outer peel and white pith from the grapefruits, then with a sharp knife cut into the fruits between the membrane to lift out the segments and reserve them.

**3** Measure the sugar into a dry saucepan. Set over a moderate heat and stir until the sugar has melted and turned to a caramel. Draw off the heat and add the grapefruit juice – cover your hand as the mixture will boil up furiously with the addition of a cold liquid.

**4** Replace the pan over the heat. Add the honey, soy sauce, lemon juice and grated root ginger. Stir until the mixture simmers and any lumps of caramel have dissolved away. Blend the cornflour with 2 tablespoons of cold water. Stir into the contents of the pan and cook, stirring until the sauce thickens and clears. Remove from the heat.

**5** Heat the oven to 200°C (400°F or gas no. 6). Set the duck breast fillets in the heated oven and cook for 30–35 minutes until the skins are golden and crisp.

**6** Reheat the sauce and add the grapefruit segments. Slice the duck breasts diagonally, place in a heated serving dish and spoon over the sauce.

# Rabbit with Mustard and Prunes

**1** The butcher will joint a rabbit for you. Spread the pieces generously with mustard and let them stand for 30–40 minutes. Peel and chop the onion, trim and snip the bacon rashers into thin strips.

**2** Heat the oven to 160°C (325°F or gas no. 3). Put the chopped onion and bacon in a dry frying pan and stir over a moderate heat until the bacon fat runs and the onion is softened. With a slotted spoon transfer the onion and bacon to a casserole.

**3** Spoon the seasoned flour onto a plate and add the dried herbs. Take the rabbit pieces and dip them in the flour mixture to coat all sides. Add the butter to the hot frying pan, add the pieces of rabbit and fry to brown them on all sides. Transfer the rabbit pieces to the casserole.

**4** Add the wine to the frying pan and stir to pick up all the flavouring bits. Pour over the rabbit. Add the stock. Cover with the casserole lid, place in the heated oven and cook for 1 hour.

**5** Combine the cream, a seasoning of salt and pepper, the grainy mustard and wine vinegar in a bowl. Stir the cream mixture into the contents of the casserole and add the prunes. Return to the oven for a further 30 minutes.

1 wild rabbit, jointed
2–3 tablespoons Dijon mustard
1 medium onion
6 streaky bacon rashers
3–4 tablespoons seasoned flour
1 teaspoon dried mixed herbs
25 g (1 oz) butter
150 ml (¼ pint) dry white wine
400 ml (¾ pint) vegetable stock
150 ml (¼ pint) double cream
salt and freshly milled pepper
1 tablespoon grainy mustard
1 teaspoon white wine vinegar
6–8 pitted tenderised prunes

**Serves 3–4**
Preparation time: 25 minutes, plus standing time
Cooking time: 1½ hours

## Katie's Tip

Dried fruits like apricots and prunes make an intriguing addition to meat and game recipes. They add colour and interest and the flavours are very compatible. Prunes go very well with rabbit and hare and are also delicious dropped into a beef casserole. Apricots are a good choice for pork or lamb stews. Soak the prunes for a few hours beforehand, or use the ready-to-eat tenderised type and add about halfway through the cooking time.

# Meat

By choosing the tender, quick-cooking meat cuts you can serve up a meal in half the usual time. What makes these dishes special are the interesting flavours used like orange juice, capers, mustard and honey or fruits. The occasional slow-cooked casserole is a great choice for weekends. While the preparation may take time, once a casserole is in the oven, it can be left to cook itself.

*Lamb with Mediterranean Vegetables*

# Lamb with Mediterranean Vegetables

1 red sweet pepper

1 yellow sweet pepper

225 g (8 oz) courgettes

1 small aubergine, about
   225 g (8 oz)

4 sun-dried tomatoes in oil

2 tablespoons oil from the jar
   of sun-dried tomatoes

4 lamb chump chops

1 tablespoon olive oil

3–4 fresh oregano sprigs (or
   1 teaspoon dried)

225 ml (8 fl oz) dry white wine

1 tablespoon concentrated
   tomato purée

1 tablespoon soft brown sugar

8 black olives

**Serves 4**

Preparation time: 10 minutes

Cooking time: 30 minutes

**1** Halve, deseed and cut the peppers into chunky pieces. Trim and slice the courgettes thickly. Cut the aubergine into chunky pieces. Fork the sun-dried tomatoes from the jar and cut each one in half.

**2** Measure the oil from the sun-dried tomatoes into a large 25 cm (10 inch) frying pan (with a lid) and set over a moderate heat. Add the lamb chops and fry to brown both sides, then remove the lamb from the pan.

**3** Add the olive oil, prepared vegetables (not the tomatoes) and the oregano. Stir and turn the vegetables in the hot drippings and fry gently for about 8 minutes.

**4** Add the sun-dried tomatoes, the wine, tomato purée and soft brown sugar. Stir and bring to a simmer. Tuck the lamb chops in among the vegetables and add the black olives. Cover with the pan lid and cook gently for 15 minutes before serving.

## Katie's Tip

Aromatic thyme, marjoram and oregano are the herbs most commonly used to pep up meat dishes. While it's great to use fresh herbs, the new freeze-dried variety are perfectly acceptable in sauced dishes. Add fresh or dried herbs at the stir-fried vegetable stage and the warmth will bring out their flavour. Remember that dried herbs are more concentrated. Allow 1 teaspoon of dried herbs for every 2–3 tablespoons of chopped fresh herbs.

# Grilled Lamb Leg Steaks with Fresh Mint Vinaigrette

**1** Lay the lamb steaks in a single layer in a shallow dish. Peel and crush the garlic. Strip the mint leaves from their stems and chop them with the sugar. Combine the olive oil and wine vinegar, then add the garlic, mint and sugar and a seasoning of freshly milled pepper. Pour the vinaigrette over the lamb steaks and leave to marinate for at least 1 hour, or until serving time.

**2** Meanwhile cream the butter until soft. Add the wine vinegar, chopped mint and a seasoning of salt and freshly milled pepper. Beat until smooth, shape into a block and chill.

**3** Preheat the grill until hot. Set the grill rack at least 7.5 cm (3 inches) from the heat source. Lift the lamb steaks from the marinade and set on the grill rack. Cook 6–8 minutes each side, basting with the remaining marinade. Serve topped with slices of the mint butter.

4 lamb leg steaks
1 clove garlic
2–3 fresh mint sprigs
1 teaspoon caster sugar
3 tablespoons olive oil
2 tablespoons white wine
  vinegar
freshly milled pepper

**FOR THE MINT BUTTER:**
50 g (2 oz) butter
1 teaspoon white wine vinegar
1 tablespoon finely chopped
  fresh mint leaves
salt and freshly milled pepper

**Serves 4**
Preparation time: 10 minutes,
  plus marinating time
Cooking time: 12–15 minutes

# Barbecued Lamb Riblets

**1** Cut the lamb between the bones into riblets and pull off the skin – this is easier to do from each individual riblet. Put lamb riblets in a large saucepan, cover with cold water and add the vinegar. Bring to a simmer for 15 minutes, then drain and let them cool.

**2** For the barbecue glaze combine the wine vinegar, brown sugar, Worcestershire sauce and tomato purée and mix well. Place lamb riblets in a single layer in an oiled roasting tin. Pour over the glaze and rub into the lamb riblets with fingers – messy but essential.

**3** Heat the oven to 180°C (350°F or gas no. 4). Set the lamb riblets in the heated oven and roast for 25–30 minutes – turn them once or twice, they will crisp up and begin to singe and caramelise when ready. Alternatively, give them less time – only 15–20 minutes – in the oven with a final crisp up on a hot barbecue.

**4** Serve the lamb riblets with hot garlic bread and a green salad.

2 breasts of lamb, with bone in
2 tablespoons white wine
  vinegar
**FOR THE BARBECUE GLAZE:**
4 tablespoons white wine
  vinegar
2 tablespoons soft brown
  sugar
1 tablespoon Worcestershire
  sauce
1 tablespoon tomato purée

**Serves 3**
Preparation time: 30 minutes,
  plus marinating time
Cooking time: 25–30 minutes

# Lamb Kebabs Flavoured with Indian Spices

**1** Trim the lamb and cut the meat into bite-sized pieces. Trim and peel the shallots leaving them whole. Blanch the shallots in boiling water for 4 minutes, then drain.

**2** For the spice mixture, measure the paprika, cumin, coriander, chilli, a seasoning of freshly milled pepper, the salt and sugar into a medium mixing bowl. Peel and crush the garlic and add along with the olive oil. Mix to make a spice paste. Add the pieces of meat and turn to coat them with the spices. Leave to marinate for at least 4 hours, to take the flavour. Toss the meat with a fork occasionally.

**3** Heat the grill until it is hot and set the grill rack at least 7.5 cm (3 inches) from the heat source. Thread the spicy lamb pieces onto 6 skewers. Set them under the heated grill to cook for 15 minutes – turning them once. Meanwhile slice the shallots in half and thread them on 3–4 separate skewers with cut faces in the same direction. Brush with olive oil (a sprinkling of caster sugar encourages browning). Set under the grill – do not turn, these will take about 6–8 minutes.

**4** Serve the spicy lamb skewers and the sweet shallots with warm pitta bread and a green salad – a bowl of seasoned yoghurt for dipping the meat pieces into would be nice.

700 g (1½ lb) boned leg of lamb
8–10 shallots
olive oil for brushing

FOR THE INDIAN SPICES:
1 tablespoon paprika
1 teaspoon ground cumin
1 teaspoon ground coriander
½ teaspoon chilli powder
freshly milled pepper
½ teaspoon salt
1 teaspoon caster sugar
2 cloves garlic
2 tablespoons olive oil

**Serves 6**
Preparation time: 25 minutes, plus marinating time
Cooking time: 15–20 minutes

# Spiced Lamb in Sweet Peppers

1 medium onion

4 cloves garlic

1 tablespoon olive oil

1 teaspoon caster sugar

700 g (1½ lb) minced lamb

1 teaspoon ground allspice

½ teaspoon ground cinnamon

1 teaspoon salt

freshly milled pepper

1 x 230 g tin chopped
tomatoes in juice

1 tablespoon concentrated
tomato purée

50 g (2 oz) seedless raisins

50 g (2 oz) pine kernels

4 yellow sweet peppers

50 g (2 oz) mature Cheddar
cheese

**Serves 4**

Preparation time: 15 minutes

Cooking time: 1 hour

**1** Peel and finely chop the onion and peel and crush the garlic. Heat the oil in a 25 cm (10 inch) frying pan, add the onion, sprinkle with the sugar and cook gently until softened and beginning to brown. Stir in the garlic.

**2** Add the minced lamb to the pan, stirring to break up the meat. Add the allspice, cinnamon, salt and a seasoning of freshly milled pepper. Stir in the contents of the tin of chopped tomatoes, the tomato purée, seedless raisins and pine kernels. Simmer gently for about 15 minutes until the meat is no longer pink.

**3** Heat the oven to 180°C (350°F or gas no. 4). Take a lengthways slice off each yellow pepper leaving the stalk intact. Remove the pepper seeds. Scald the peppers for 3 minutes in boiling water, then drain. Pack peppers in a casserole dish large enough to hold them all on a single layer.

**4** Spoon the meat filling into the pepper shells, packing it in gently. Add 2–3 tablespoons water to the casserole dish. Cover with the casserole lid. Set the dish in the preheated oven and bake for 30–40 minutes. Uncover and top the peppers with thin slices (or grated) cheese and return to the oven for 5 minutes more until the cheese is melted and just bubbling.

# Roast Lamb with Garlic and Rosemary

**1** Trim the lamb fillets and cut each one in half (butchers usually sell them whole, in supermarket packs they are often already cut). Rub the lamb fillets with 1 tablespoon of the olive oil and rub in the cracked pepper (sometimes called steak pepper).

**2** Heat the oven to 180°C (350°F or gas no. 4). Scrub the new potatoes leaving on the skins. Remove the outer papery coating from the heads of garlic but leave the heads whole with root intact. Cut the potatoes across in thin slices, turn them in 1 tablespoon of the remaining olive oil and season with salt and freshly milled pepper. Turn the potatoes into a roasting tin and spread. Rub the garlic heads with your oily fingers and pull heads open gently. Place the garlic in the roasting tin.

**3** Heat the remaining tablespoon of olive oil in a frying pan, add the lamb and fry to seal and brown them – about 4–5 minutes. Arrange the browned lamb fillets in the roasting tin on top of the potatoes. Add rosemary sprigs. Set in the hot oven and roast for 40 minutes.

**4** Serve the lamb sliced (at an angle, like French bread), with the potatoes and pieces of the sweet, soft heads of garlic.

2 lamb neck fillets, trimmed
3 tablespoons olive oil
2 teaspoons cracked pepper
500 g (18 oz) new potatoes
2 garlic heads
salt and freshly milled pepper
2–3 fresh rosemary sprigs

**Serves 4–6**

Preparation time: 25 minutes
Cooking time: 40 minutes

# Pork Loin Steaks with Apple and Cider

**1** Chose a baking dish that looks good enough to bring to the table. Heat the oil and half the butter in a frying pan. Add the pork loin steaks and turn to brown them on both sides. Remove from the pan. Deglaze the hot pan with about 4 tablespoons of cold water, stir well to pick up the coagulated pan juices and reserve them.

**2** Heat the oven to 190°C (375°F or gas no. 5). Peel and thinly slice the apples and onions. Arrange these over the base of a buttered 1.1 litre (2 pint) baking dish. Sprinkle with the sugar and sage and set the pork loin steaks on top in a single layer. Season with salt and pepper. Pour over the reserved deglazing liquid and add the cider.

**3** In a mixing bowl combine the fresh breadcrumbs, the grated cheese and the chopped parsley. Sprinkle the breadcrumb mixture over the top of the meat to cover. Top with the remaining butter cut in flakes. Place the dish in the heated oven and cook for 1 hour. Serve from the baking dish – the apples and onion should be soft and juicy and the topping should be crisp and golden.

1 tablespoon grapeseed oil
50 g (2 oz) butter
4 pork loin steaks
2 medium cooking apples
2 medium onions
1 tablespoon caster sugar
½ teaspoon dried sage
salt and freshly milled pepper
150 ml (¼ pint) dry cider
75 g (3 oz) fresh white or
    wholemeal breadcrumbs
50 g (2 oz) grated hard cheese
2 tablespoons chopped fresh
    parsley

**Serves 4**

Preparation time: 30 minutes
Cooking time: 1 hour

# Pork Chops with Green Beans in Mustard Caper Sauce

4 boneless pork loin chops

350 g (12 oz) French beans

1 tablespoon olive oil

175 ml (6 fl oz) vegetable
 stock

1 tablespoon white wine
 vinegar

2 tablespoons capers

150 ml (¼ pint) double cream

2 tablespoons Dijon mustard

salt and freshly milled pepper

**Serves 4**

Preparation time: 15 minutes

Cooking time: 35 minutes

**1** Trim the pork chops, cutting off any rind and some of the fat. Top and tail the French beans and cut into 2.5 cm (1 inch) lengths. Heat the oil in a large 25 cm (10 inch) frying pan (with a lid). Add the pork and fry turning to brown well – about 8 minutes. Then remove from the pan.

**2** Pour off excess drippings. Add the stock and white wine vinegar and bring to a simmer, stirring to scrape off any brown bits. Stir in the well-drained capers. Replace the pork chops, cover with the pan lid and simmer gently for 15 minutes. Add the green beans, replace the lid and simmer for a further 5 minutes.

**3** In a bowl combine the cream and mustard and add salt and pepper. Add to the pork. Stir and bring back to a simmer to serve.

# Pork Fillet with Fruit and Honey Mustard Glaze

2 plump pork fillets, about
 350 g (12 oz) each

4 tablespoons olive oil

1 teaspoon cracked pepper

225 g (8 oz) ready-to-eat
 dried apricots or prunes

2 tablespoons clear honey

2 tablespoons Dijon mustard

salt and freshly milled pepper

**Serves 4–6**

Preparation time: 20 minutes

Cooking time: 30–45 minutes

**1** Trim the pork fillets of all membrane and skin. Rub all over with no more than 2 tablespoons of olive oil and cracked pepper.

**2** Slice the pork fillets lengthways but not completely in half. Stuff the slit in each pork fillet with dried apricots or prunes. Then, with a good length of fine string, tie each pork fillet closed, to hold the shape of the meat piece. In a mixing bowl combine the remaining olive oil, honey and mustard, and season with salt and freshly milled pepper.

**3** Heat the oven to 200°C (400°F or gas no. 6). Place the fillets in a roasting tin and set in the heated oven for 20 minutes. Pour over the honey mustard glaze and baste the meat. Return to the oven for a further 10–15 minutes, basting several times to achieve a golden glaze.

**4** Snip and remove the string. Serve the pork sliced on the diagonal, to reveal the fruit filling, with the glaze from the tin. To serve cold, take the pork fillets out of the tin and cool before removing string, then slice.

# Casserole of Pork Shoulder with Sweet Onions and Apricots

*This would go very well with something unusual like couscous or saffron rice.*

**1** Heat the oven to 160°C (325°F or gas no. 3). Cut the pork shoulder into bite-sized pieces (buy diced pork if you prefer). Peel, halve and slice the onions. Pare the carrot, cut lengthways into quarters and crossways into sticks.

**2** Combine the flour, a seasoning of salt and milled pepper and the allspice on a plate. Dip the pork pieces to coat them in the seasoned flour. Heat 2 tablespoons of the olive oil in a large 25 cm (10 inch) frying pan. Add the pork pieces (in batches) and fry to seal them on all sides. With a slotted spoon transfer the pork to a casserole. Add the carrots and dried apricots to the pork pieces.

**3** Add the remaining olive oil to the frying pan and add the sliced onions. Sprinkle with the sugar and fry the onions gently for about 10 minutes, stirring occasionally until the onions are soft and golden brown. Stir in the oregano. Draw off the heat and stir in the vinegar along with 2 tablespoons water. Stir to pick up all the flavouring bits and tip the contents of the pan into the casserole.

**4** In a measuring jug combine the concentrated tomato purée, vegetable stock and vermouth. Stir and pour into the casserole. Cover, place in the heated oven and cook for 1½ hours until the meat is tender. Finely chop the pared lemon rind and combine with the parsley. Scatter over the casserole before serving.

700–900 g (1½–2 lb) boneless shoulder pork
2 large onions
350 g (12 oz) carrots
3 tablespoons plain flour
salt and freshly milled pepper
½ teaspoon ground allspice
3 tablespoons olive oil
75 g (3 oz) ready-to-eat dried apricots
1 teaspoon caster sugar
1 teaspoon dried oregano
2 tablespoons white wine vinegar
3 tablespoons concentrated tomato purée
400 ml (¾ pint) vegetable stock
75 ml (3 fl oz) dry white vermouth
2–3 pieces pared lemon rind
2 tablespoons chopped fresh parsley

**Serves 6**
Preparation time: 40 minutes
Cooking time: 1½ hours

# Spiced Pork Medallions with Flageolet Beans

700 g (1½ lb) pork fillet
1 medium onion
1 tablespoon plain flour
2 teaspoons paprika
2 tablespoons olive oil
4–6 whole fresh sage leaves
150 ml (¼ pint) vegetable
  stock
75 ml (3 fl oz) dry white
  vermouth
1 x 400 g tin flageolet beans
salt and freshly milled pepper
3 tablespoons double cream

**Serves 4**

Preparation time: 20 minutes
Cooking time: 30–35 minutes

**1** Trim the pork fillet, then cut the meat across the grain into 1 cm (½ inch) slices. Peel and finely chop the onion.

**2** Measure the flour and paprika into a roomy polythene bag. Add the pieces of meat and shake to coat them all over. Turn the meat onto a plate and shake off any loose flour.

**3** Heat the olive oil in a large 25 cm (10 inch) frying pan (with a lid). Add the pork pieces and fry to brown them – the paprika will encourage them to take on a golden colour. Give them 5–6 minutes over a moderate heat and they will be almost cooked. Lift the pork from the pan.

**4** Add the chopped onion to the hot pan drippings. Stir and let it soften and take a little colour. Stir in the sage leaves. Then add the stock and vermouth and bring to a simmer.

**5** Meanwhile drain the flageolet beans and add them to the pan. Return the pork pieces and add a seasoning of salt and freshly milled pepper. Bring to a simmer, cover with the pan lid and let the contents cook gently for about 10 minutes. Add the spoonfuls of cream just before serving.

# Pork Satays with Peanut Dip

450 g (1 lb) lean pork fillet
3 tablespoons soy sauce
1 tablespoon lemon juice
1 tablespoon soft brown sugar
1 small onion
2 cloves garlic
1 tablespoon grapeseed oil
1 teaspoon mild chilli powder
2 heaped tablespoons crunchy
  peanut butter

**Serves 4**

Preparation time: 20 minutes,
  plus marinating time
Cooking time: 12–15 minutes

**1** Trim the pork fillet, then hold the knife at an angle and cut into thin slices. In a mixing bowl, combine the soy sauce, lemon juice and sugar. Add the meat pieces and turn in the marinade. Cover and refrigerate for at least 4 hours.

**2** Drain the pork pieces, reserving the marinade. Peel and finely chop the onion. Peel the garlic and crush. Heat the oil in a saucepan, add the onion and fry until soft. Add the garlic and chilli powder and fry for a few moments more. Add the peanut butter and 175 ml (6 fl oz) water. Stir until the mixture comes to a simmer and thickens. Cook gently for 2–3 minutes. Stir in the reserved marinade and bring back to a simmer.

**3** Meanwhile, thread 4–5 pieces of pork onto each of 8 soaked bamboo skewers. Grill for 12 minutes turning them halfway through the grilling time. Serve with steamed rice. Pass the sauce round in a bowl and let guests take a spoonful or two as a dipping sauce for the pork pieces.

# Swedish Meatballs in Soured Cream

2 slices white bread

3–4 tablespoons milk

1 small onion

700 g (1½ lb) extra lean
  minced beef

salt and freshly milled pepper

grated nutmeg

2 eggs

25–50 g (1–2 oz) butter

600 ml (1 pint) vegetable
  stock

1 tablespoon grainy mustard

300 ml (½ pint) soured cream
  or natural yoghurt

2 tablespoons cornflour

caraway seeds or chopped
  fresh parsley to garnish

**Serves 4**

Preparation time: 20 minutes,
  plus chilling time

Cooking time: 1 hour

**1** Trim the crusts from the bread slices and break the white part into a mixing bowl. Add the milk to moisten and mix with a fork to break up the crumbs. Peel and finely chop or grate the onion.

**2** Add the minced beef, onion, a seasoning of salt and freshly milled pepper, a good grating of nutmeg and the eggs to the bowl. Mix the ingredients very thoroughly. Shape into about 48 small meatballs. Chill for 2 hours to firm them up.

**3** Melt 25 g (1 oz) of the butter in a large 25 cm (10 inch) frying pan. When frothing and hot, add a batch of half the meatballs. Shake the pan to keep them moving and cook until browned all over. With a slotted spoon transfer to a casserole. Add the remaining meatballs with extra butter as needed and repeat the process until all the meatballs are browned.

**4** Heat the oven to 180°C (350°F or gas no. 4). Add the stock to the hot frying pan. Stir to pick up any flavouring bits and bring to the boil. Strain over the meatballs. Stir in the mustard, cover with the casserole lid. Set in the heated oven and cook for 45 minutes.

**5** In a bowl combine the soured cream (or yoghurt) and cornflour. Stir gently through the contents of the casserole and return to the oven (uncovered) for a further 15 minutes until bubbling hot – the sauce will thicken. Sprinkle with caraway seeds or chopped parsley and serve.

---

### Katie's Tip

To get perfect meatballs use wet (not floured) fingers
to shape them. Fingers dipped in flour quickly become
sticky, a small bowl of water at your side is all you need.
Use wetted hands for pressing and patting meatloaf
or for shaping hamburgers too.

# Marinated Roast Beef with Onion Marmalade

*Your piece of meat should be ready rolled and tied for roasting. Dry the outside well with kitchen paper.*

**1** For the dry marinade, combine the salt, pepper, mustard powder, celery seasoning, dried thyme and ground cloves in a bowl. Peel and finely chop the garlic and add to the mixture. Rub the outside of the joint well with the dry, spicy blend – you won't need it all but it keeps well and can be used another time. Wrap the joint in greaseproof paper and refrigerate overnight or better still for 48 hours.

**2** Combine the oil, red wine vinegar and tomato purée for the wet marinade. Unwrap the beef joint and place in a large freezer bag. Add the marinade and tie the bag closed. Leave the meat to marinate in the refrigerator for up to 24 hours, turning the bag once or twice to keep the meat moist.

**3** Heat the oven to 220°C (425°F or gas no. 7). Lift the meat from the bag and reserve the marinade mixture in a bowl for basting. Set the beef joint in a roasting tin – no dripping or fat is required – place in the heated oven and roast for 20 minutes. Reduce the oven heat to 180°C (350°F or gas no. 4) for the rest of the cooking time. Allow 20 minutes per 450 g (1 lb) for rare and 25 minutes per 450 g (1 lb) for medium done. Spoon over a little of the reserved marinade during roasting. When cooked the outside should be crusty and brown with the inside still a little pink

**4** Let the joint stand for 10 minutes so meat juices settle before carving. Serve with Onion Marmalade as a relish.

**Onion Marmalade:** Peel 900 g (2 lb) large onions and slice them thinly. Peel and crush 2 cloves garlic. Into a large 25 cm (10 inch) frying pan (with a lid) measure 150 ml (¼ pint) water, then add 75 ml (3 fl oz) red wine, 2 tablespoons red wine vinegar, 4 tablespoons soft brown sugar, the sliced onions, crushed garlic and a seasoning of salt and freshly milled pepper. Bring the contents to a boil. Stir, then reduce the heat to a gentle simmer. Cover the pan and cook for 30 minutes or until the onions are well softened. Remove pan lid and cook, stirring occasionally, until the onion mixture is thick and brown. Allow to cool before serving. Onion marmalade will keep in the refrigerator for up to 1 week.

1 piece rolled topside or silverside of beef, about 2.5 kg (5 lb)
Onion Marmalade (recipe below)

FOR THE DRY MARINADE:
50 g (2 oz) salt
1 tablespoon ground black pepper
1 tablespoon mustard powder
1 tablespoon celery seasoning
½ tablespoon dried thyme
½ tablespoon ground cloves
2 cloves garlic

FOR THE WET MARINADE:
150 ml (5 fl oz) grapeseed or other light oil
150 ml (5 fl oz) red wine vinegar
2 tablespoons concentrated tomato purée

**Serves 12**
Preparation time: 40 minutes, plus marinating time
Cooking time: 2–2½ hours

# Beef Stew with Parsley Dumplings

700 g (1½ lb) lean braising
  steak
5–6 tablespoons seasoned
  flour
6–8 small button onions
4 carrots
3 parsnips
2 tablespoons olive oil
1 tablespoon concentrated
  tomato purée
600 ml (1 pint) vegetable
  stock
150 ml (¼ pint) red wine or
  cider
2 slivers pared orange rind
2 bay leaves
1 teaspoon red wine vinegar

FOR THE DUMPLINGS:

50 g (2 oz) self-raising flour
salt and freshly milled pepper
25 g (1 oz) shredded beef suet
1 tablespoon chopped fresh
  parsley

**1** Trim the meat and cut into bite-sized pieces. Toss in the seasoned flour. Peel the onions, leaving them whole. Pare the carrots and parsnips and cut into batons.

**2** Heat the oil in a large 25 cm (10 inch) frying pan, add the onions and fry, turning to brown them a little. With a slotted spoon, transfer the onions to a casserole dish. In batches, add the pieces of meat to the hot pan drippings. Turn the pieces to seal and brown them and add to the casserole with the carrot and parsnip batons.

**3** Heat the oven to 160°C (325°F or gas no. 3). Stir the tomato purée into the hot vegetable stock. Add the red wine or cider to the frying pan and stir to pick up all the flavouring bits. Pour this over the meat and vegetables. Add the stock, pared orange rind, bay leaves and red wine vinegar. Cover with the lid. Set in the heated oven and cook for 2 hours or until the meat is tender.

**4** About 20 minutes before the end of the cooking time, prepare the dumplings. Sift the flour into a mixing bowl, add a seasoning of salt and pepper, the suet and parsley. Add sufficient cold water – about 2–3 tablespoons – and mix with a fork to make a soft scone dough. Divide the mixture into quarters. With floured fingers roll each piece into a ball.

**5** Uncover the casserole and add the dumplings, setting them on top of the meat and vegetables. Re-cover and replace in the oven for a further 20 minutes.

**Serves 4**
Preparation time: 30 minutes
Cooking time: 2 hours

## Katie's Tip

A dash of wine vinegar improves the taste of any casserole
by sharpening up the flavour. It cuts through a rich gravy or
sauce and makes a big difference. You rarely need much
more than a teaspoon stirred in with the ingredients or at the
end – it's like seasoning.

# Teriyaki Steaks with Fresh Pineapple

6 beef fillet steaks
2 tablespoons soft brown
  sugar
2 tablespoons soy sauce
juice 1 lemon
2 tablespoons grapeseed or
  other light oil
1 teaspoon grated fresh ginger
salt and freshly milled pepper
25 g (1 oz) butter
150 ml (¼ pint) red wine
3 tablespoons redcurrant jelly
4 rings fresh pineapple

**Serves 6**

Preparation time: 15 minutes,
  plus marinating time
Cooking time: 15 minutes

**1** Trim the steaks and place in a single layer in a shallow dish. Combine the soft brown sugar, soy sauce, lemon juice, grapeseed oil, grated fresh ginger and a seasoning of salt and pepper and pour over the steaks. Cover and refrigerate for at least 4 hours or overnight, turning the steaks once or twice.

**2** Melt the butter in a large 25 cm (10 inch) frying pan. Lift the steaks from the marinade, add to the hot butter and fry (5 minutes for rare, 6–8 minutes for medium done) turning them once or twice. Lift the steaks from the pan and keep hot.

**3** Pour the red wine into the hot pan and bring to a simmer, stir to pick up any flavouring bits. Add the strained marinade and the redcurrant jelly. Stir to melt the jelly. Cut the pineapple rings into chunky pieces. Add the pineapple to the pan and heat for a moment. Spoon the sauce and pineapple pieces over the steaks and then serve.

# Lamb Chops with Pumpkin

2 racks of lamb, chine bone
  removed
700–900 g (1½–2 lb) pumpkin
  or butternut squash
FOR THE HONEY GLAZE:
2 tablespoons clear honey
pared rind and juice 1 lemon
3 tablespoons olive oil
1 tablespoon Worcestershire
  sauce
1 teaspoon Dijon mustard
salt and freshly milled pepper
2–3 fresh thyme sprigs

**Serves 4–6**

Preparation time: 20 minutes
Cooking time: 35–40 minutes

**1** Cut into the racks of lamb between each bone to get long rib bones each with a small eye of meat. Cut away the excess fat, then arrange the rib eye chops in a single layer in a shallow dish. Pare or cut away the outer rind from the pumpkin or squash, scoop out and reserve the inner seeds. Cut the pumpkin or squash into chunks.

**2** In a bowl combine the honey, 2–3 pieces pared lemon rind, the squeezed lemon juice, olive oil and Worcestershire sauce. Add the mustard, a seasoning of salt and pepper and a sprinkling of fresh thyme sprigs and mix well. Pour the glaze over the lamb chops, turn to coat them in the glaze and let them marinate until serving time.

**3** Heat the oven to 200°C (400°F or gas no. 6). Place the pieces of pumpkin or squash in an oiled roasting tin – large enough to take all the chops too. Season with salt and pepper and set in the heated oven for 10 minutes. Then add the rib eye chops and all the honey glaze from the dish. Return to the oven and cook for 25–30 minutes or until the chops are glazed and golden and the pumpkin or squash is tender. If the pumpkin or squash are omitted reduce cooking time to 15–20 minutes. If you like, stir-fry a few of the reserved pumpkin or squash seeds in olive oil, sprinkle with salt and use as a garnish.

# Spiced Pears for Cold Meats

*These look mouthwatering arranged around the rim of a platter of cold turkey, chicken or ham.*

**1** Heat the oven to 160°C (325°F or gas no. 3). Peel and halve the pears – leave on the stalks as they look pretty. Using a teaspoon, carefully scoop out the core from each half and then place the pear halves in a casserole.

**2** Measure the soft brown sugar and red wine vinegar into a saucepan. Slice the lemon thinly and add. Cut the ginger into slivers and lightly crush the allspice berries. Add to the pan along with the piece of stick cinnamon. Bring to a simmer, stirring to dissolve the sugar and pour over the pears.

**3** Cover with the casserole lid. Set in the heated oven and bake for 40 minutes until the pears are tender – test with a knife tip. Let the pears cool, then transfer to a lidded container and store in the refrigerator. These will keep for 1–2 weeks. Fork pears from the syrup to serve.

700 g (1½ lb) hard Conference pears
225 g (8 oz) soft brown sugar
175 ml (6 fl oz) red wine vinegar
1 lemon
2.5 cm (1 inch) pared fresh ginger
1 teaspoon whole allspice
2.5 cm (1 inch) stick cinnamon

### Serves 8–10

Preparation time: 20 minutes, plus cooling time
Cooking time: 40 minutes

---

### STARS OF THE EAST

Subtly spiced rice is a great standby, add a few simple ingredients for great flavours.

**Aromatic:** Pare and coarsely grate 2.5 cm (1 inch) fresh ginger. Take seeds from 6 cardamom pods. Heat 1 tablespoon oil, add the ginger and heat for 1 minute. Stir in the cardamom seeds, 225 g (8 oz) long grain rice, 1 teaspoon ground turmeric, 25 g (1 oz) currants, 4 whole cloves and 2.5 cm (1 inch) stick cinnamon. Stir for 1 minute. Add 600 ml (1 pint) hot vegetable stock. Cover and simmer for 15 minutes. Fork in 15 g (½ oz) butter before serving.

**Five spice:** Peel and crush 2 garlic cloves. Pare and grate 2.5 cm (1 inch) fresh ginger. Heat 1 tablespoon oil, add the garlic and ginger. Heat for 1 minute. Add 6 crushed peppercorns, 225 g (8 oz) long grain rice, 2 star anise (pictured), 4 cloves and 2.5 cm (1 inch) stick cinnamon. Add 600 ml (1 pint) hot stock. Simmer for 15 minutes. Fork in 15 g (½ oz) butter.

# Seafood

Fish needs only modest preparation complemented with the simplest of ingredients to produce something really spectacular for just about any kind of meal. Fish cooks quickly and can be teamed with herbs, flavoured butters, oriental dressings or salsas. Whole fish cooked on the bone has a sweeter fuller flavour, or it can be cut into steaks, which makes serving easier.

*Prawn Jambalaya*

# Prawn Jambalaya

50 g (2 oz) streaky bacon
  rashers
1 medium onion
2 cloves garlic
1 green sweet pepper
1 teaspoon paprika
1 teaspoon chilli powder
175 g (6 oz) long grain rice
1 x 397 g tin chopped
  tomatoes
400 ml (¾ pint) vegetable
  stock
225 g (8 oz) ham, cut in thick
  slices
2 chorizos – spicy sausages
100 g (4 oz) cooked and
  peeled king prawns
salt and freshly milled pepper
dash of Tabasco sauce
lemon halves to serve

**Serves 4**
Preparation time: 25 minutes
Cooking time: 25–30 minutes

**1** Snip away the rind, then coarsely cut up the streaky bacon rashers. Put the bacon pieces  in a large 25 cm (10 inch) frying pan (with a lid) and fry gently until the fat runs from the bacon. Meanwhile peel and finely slice the onion and peel and crush the garlic. Halve, deseed and cut the green pepper into chunky pieces, removing the stalk.

**2** Add the onion to the frying pan and cook gently to soften. Stir in the paprika and the chilli powder and stir over the heat for a moment. Stir in the crushed garlic, cut up green pepper and the rice and cook, stirring for 2 minutes.

**3** Stir in the contents of the can of tomatoes and the vegetable stock and mix well. Bring to the boil, lower the heat to a simmer. Cut the ham into chunky pieces and slice the chorizos and add both to the pan. Cover with the frying pan lid and then cook gently for 25–30 minutes or until the rice grains are tender and all the liquid has been absorbed.

**4** Add the prawns, a good seasoning of salt and milled pepper and a dash of Tabasco. Heat through for a moment, then serve with halves of lemon to squeeze over.

# Smoked Fish Coulibiac

**1** Poach the smoked haddock in 600 ml (1 pint) cold water with half the lemon, cut in slices, and the bay leaves until the fish is tender – about 6 minutes. Break the flesh into loose flakes, discarding the skin and any bones. Taste the poaching liquor for seasoning. Strain and reserve 400 ml (¾ pint) for cooking the rice. Cut the mushrooms into chunky pieces.

**2** Peel and finely chop the onion. Put 25 g (1 oz) butter in a medium saucepan, add the onion and sauté gently to soften. Add the curry powder and the rice and mix. Stir in the reserved poaching liquor and bring to a simmer, then cover with the pan lid and cook until the rice has absorbed the liquid – about 20 minutes. Allow the rice to cool. Meanwhile melt the remaining butter in a frying pan, add the mushrooms and toss over the heat for a few minutes. Using a fork, fold the fish and mushrooms into the rice along with the squeezed juice of the remaining lemon half. Fold in the soured cream to moisten the mixture.

**3** On a floured board roll out one piece of pastry to a rectangle approximately 30 x 10 cm (12 x 4 inches) – adjust the size to the length of your baking sheet if necessary. Trim the edges straight with a knife and set the pastry on the baking sheet. Roll the remaining pastry to a similar length but half as wide again (to take in the filling) and trim the edges straight. Lightly flour this pastry strip and fold in half lengthways, then cut a series of slits along the folded side to within 1 cm (½ inch) of the trimmed edges. Spoon the rice mixture onto the pastry base, heaping it up to get a domed ridge, and leave a clear 1 cm (½ inch) around the border. Brush the border with lightly beaten egg. Open out the pastry top and place it over the filling, pressing the edges together to seal all around. Refrigerate the coulibiac until ready to bake, then remove 30 minutes before to lose the chill.

**4** Heat the oven to 200°C (400°F or gas no. 6). Brush the pastry top with lightly beaten egg. Bake the coulibiac for 20 minutes (when the pastry should be beginning to brown), then reduce the oven temperature to 190°C (375°F or gas no. 5) and cook for another 20 minutes. Warm the butter until melted, stir in 1 tablespoon snipped coriander leaves. Serve the coulibiac cut in thick slices with the coriander butter drizzled over.

900 g (2 lb) smoked haddock
  fillet
1 lemon
2 bay leaves
salt and freshly milled pepper
225 g (8 oz) chestnut or
  brown cap mushrooms
1 medium onion
50 g (2 oz) butter
2 teaspoons curry powder
175 g (6 oz) long grain rice
400 ml (¾ pint) poached fish
  liquor – see method
2–3 tablespoons soured cream
2 x 250 g packets frozen puff
  pastry, thawed
1 lightly beaten egg
75–100 g (3–4 oz) unsalted
  butter and fresh coriander
  leaves to serve

**Serves 8**
Preparation time: 50 minutes,
  plus cooling time
Cooking time: 40 minutes

# Scallops in a Cream and Curry Sauce

1 medium onion

1 clove garlic

2 thin slices pared fresh ginger

1 tablespoon oil

1 tablespoon mild curry paste

400 ml (¾ pint) vegetable
stock

1 teaspoon tomato purée

1 tablespoon mango chutney

50 g (2 oz) creamed coconut

juice ½ lemon

6 fresh scallops

225 g (8 oz) cooked and
peeled tiger prawns

2 rings fresh pineapple

50 g (2 oz) butter

2–3 tablespoons double cream

**Serves 4**

Preparation time: 25–30 minutes

Cooking time: 15 minutes

**1** Peel and finely chop the onion, peel and crush the garlic and finely chop the fresh root ginger. Heat the oil in a saucepan, add the onion and fry gently to soften. Stir in the garlic and fresh ginger and cook for a moment more. Stir in the curry paste.

**2** Stir in the vegetable stock, add the tomato purée, the mango chutney (chop any large pieces of fruit) and the crumbled coconut cream. Bring the sauce to the boil, stirring until thickened. Simmer gently for 5 minutes, then draw off the heat and add the lemon juice. Taste for flavour.

**3** Trim the scallops by pulling away any membrane. If yours have roes attached, detach them gently, keeping each roe whole. Slice the scallops into 2–3 thick pieces. If the prawns are frozen, make sure they are thawed and pour off any juices. Cut the pineapple into small pieces.

**4** Melt the butter in a large 25 cm (10 inch) frying pan. Add the scallop pieces and fry gently for 1–2 minutes, then add the scallop roes and cook for about 1 minute. Add the pineapple pieces and the prawns and mix gently. Then pour in the curry sauce and bring to a simmer. Stir in the cream, heat for a moment longer, then draw off the heat. Serve with buttered basmati rice.

# Baked Sea Bass with Tomatoes, Potatoes and Onion

**1** Heat the oven to 190°C (375°F or gas no. 5). Rub the fish over with a little of the olive oil and lay in a roomy baking dish or roasting tin.

**2** With a knife tip cut out and discard the stalk end of each tomato. Scald the tomatoes in boiling water for a few moments, then skin, halve and discard the seeds. Chop the tomato flesh coarsely. Peel, halve and finely slice the onion. Peel and crush the garlic.

**3** Heat the olive oil in a saucepan, add the onion and soften for a few moments. Stir in the crushed garlic, add the tomatoes, salt and pepper, a pinch of sugar, the herbes de Provence, bay leaves and the white wine and bring to a simmer. Remove from the heat.

**4** Meanwhile peel and thinly slice the potatoes. Add the potatoes to the tomato mixture and pour the contents of the pan over the fish. Spread evenly over the baking dish. Set in the preheated oven and bake for 35–40 minutes. When cooked the fish and vegetables will be tender and there will be very little liquid left. Lift the sea bass from the bones and serve with the vegetable mixture.

1 sea bass, about 700 g (1½ lb)
2–3 tablespoons olive oil
500 g (18 oz) ripe tomatoes
1 medium onion
2 cloves garlic
salt and freshly milled pepper
pinch of sugar
1 teaspoon herbes de Provence
2 bay leaves
200 ml (7 fl oz) dry white wine
500 g (18 oz) maincrop potatoes

**Serves 2**
Preparation time: 20 minutes
Cooking time: 35–40 minutes

# Stuffed Roast Sea Bass

**1** Using about 1 tablespoon of the olive oil, lightly oil a large baking dish (or roasting tin) and rub the sea bass all over. Place the fish in the baking dish, season with sea salt and tuck fresh thyme sprigs alongside. Combine the remaining olive oil and balsamic vinegar.

**2** In a mixing bowl combine the breadcrumbs, chopped parsley, thyme and a seasoning of salt and pepper for the stuffing. Peel and finely chop the garlic. Add the chopped garlic, grated lemon rind and stir in the olive oil to moisten. Pack the stuffing into the body cavity of each fish.

**3** Heat the oven to 220°C (425°F or gas no. 7). Pour the olive oil and balsamic vinegar mixture over the stuffed sea bass. Set the fish in the heated oven and bake for 20–25 minutes, basting from time to time. Serve from the baking dish.

6 tablespoons olive oil
2 sea bass, each about 700–900 g (1½–2 lb)
sea salt
fresh thyme sprigs
1 tablespoon balsamic vinegar
FOR THE STUFFING:
100 g (4 oz)  breadcrumbs
4 tablespoons chopped fresh parsley
1 tablespoon chopped fresh thyme
salt and freshly milled pepper
2 cloves garlic
rind 1 lemon
3 tablespoons olive oil

**Serves 4–6**
Preparation time: 15 minutes
Cooking time: 20–25 minutes

# Pan-Fried Salmon with Summer Vegetables

*This should be cooked right at the last minute and served immediately.*

225 g (8 oz) salmon fillet

1½ tablespoons cornflour

salt and freshly milled pepper

100 g (4 oz) baby sweetcorn

100 g (4 oz) mangetout

3–4 spring onions

1 tablespoon caster sugar

1 tablespoon dark soy sauce

1 tablespoon dry sherry

2 teaspoons white wine
  vinegar

1 teaspoon grated fresh ginger

50 ml (2 fl oz) vegetable stock

2 tablespoons grapeseed oil

**Serves 2**

Preparation time: 20 minutes

Cooking time: 12–15 minutes

**1** Buy this salmon piece in one portion and have the skin removed from the underside. Cut the fish across in 2.5 cm (1 inch) strips. Measure the cornflour onto a sheet of greaseproof paper and season with salt and freshly milled pepper. Add the salmon pieces and toss gently to coat them on all sides. Remove the salmon and tip the remaining seasoned cornflour (about 2 teaspoons) into a small bowl.

**2** Slice the baby sweetcorn lengthways. Top and tail the mangetout. Trim the spring onions and cut both white and green stems diagonally into 2.5 cm (1 inch) pieces. Add 1 tablespoon of cold water to the seasoned cornflour and stir until smooth. Add the sugar, soy sauce, dry sherry, white wine vinegar, ginger and stock and stir to mix.

**3** Heat half the oil in a frying pan or wok. Add the salmon pieces and cook, turning gently until they are browned. Remove from the pan with a slotted spoon and keep hot. Add the remaining oil to the pan and stir in the sweetcorn, mangetout and spring onions. Cook stirring constantly for 2–3 minutes. Add 2 tablespoons water, cover and cook 3–4 minutes until vegetables are tender – shake the pan once or twice.

**4** Stir up the cornflour mixture and pour over the vegetables. Add the salmon pieces. Turn the salmon and vegetables to coat them with the glaze as the sauce comes to the boil and thickens. Serve hot.

# Monkfish and Bacon Kebabs

**1** Cut the monkfish fillets across into chunky pieces.

**2** Combine the olive oil, lemon juice and cracked pepper (also called steak pepper) in a bowl. Add the fish pieces, turn to coat, then chill for an hour or until cooking time.

**3** Trim the bacon and stretch each rasher by pressing with a knife blade along the chopping board. Cut the rashers in half. Lift the monkfish pieces from the marinade and wrap each one in a piece of bacon. Fix several on each of six satay sticks.

**4** Grill for 8–10 minutes, turning them halfway through the cooking time. Serve with Fresh Tomato and Ginger Chutney.

**Fresh Tomato and Ginger Chutney:** Skin, half and seed 450 g (1 lb) ripe tomatoes. Coarsely chop the flesh and place in a saucepan with 75 g (3 oz) caster sugar, 1 crushed clove garlic, 2.5 cm (1 inch) fresh ginger, chopped, 75 g (3 oz) sultanas, ½ teaspoon salt and a seasoning of freshly milled pepper. Simmer uncovered for about 20 minutes until the mixture is the consistency of a soft chutney. Add lemon juice to taste, then cool.

4 monkfish fillets

75 ml (3 fl oz) olive oil

2 tablespoons lemon juice

2 teaspoons cracked black pepper (also called steak pepper)

225 g (8 oz) streaky bacon rashers

Fresh Tomato and Ginger Chutney to serve (recipe below)

**Serves 6**

Preparation time: 15 minutes, plus marinating time

Cooking time: 8–10 minutes

SEAFOOD

123

# Monkfish, Squid and Mussels in Tomato and Garlic Dressing

**1** Cut the monkfish fillets across in 2.5 cm (1 inch) pieces. Rinse the squid and detach the head of each body and gently pull it away with all its attachments. Draw out the transparent 'fin' bone. Slice the body across into thin rings.

**2** Heat the oil in a large 25 cm (10 inch) frying pan. Add the pieces of monkfish in two batches frying them for 3–5 minutes, turning the pieces frequently to prevent them sticking. When white and firm, transfer to a large bowl. Add the squid rings to the pan and fry, stirring to keep them moving, for about 2 minutes or until opaque and firm. Add the squid to the monkfish pieces. Add the cooked mussels to the bowl along with the sun-dried tomatoes, drained from any oil and cut into slivers.

**3** For the dressing, combine the lemon rind and juice, sun-dried tomato paste, a seasoning of salt and pepper, the parsley and oil in a bowl. Peel and crush the garlic and add. Taste for flavour and pour the dressing over the seafood. Marinate for 1–2 hours. Then turn onto a platter and add a lemon slice or two for serving.

4 monkfish fillets
300 g (11 oz) squid
3 tablespoons olive oil
250 g (9 oz) cooked mussels
3–4 sun-dried tomatoes, in oil
lemon slices to serve
FOR THE DRESSING:
rind and juice 1 lemon
2 teaspoons sun-dried tomato
  paste
salt and freshly milled pepper
2 tablespoons chopped parsley
100 ml (4 fl oz) olive oil
2 cloves garlic

**Serves 6**

Preparation time: 20 minutes,
  plus marinating time
Cooking time: 10 minutes

# Hake with Browned Onions

**1** Have the fishmonger remove the skin from the fish fillets. Cut the fish into 4 serving portions. Season each piece with salt and freshly milled pepper and place the fish in an oiled baking dish. Peel and finely chop the onion and peel and crush the garlic.

**2** Heat the oil in a frying pan, add the onion and fry gently until soft and a little golden. Add the garlic and stir. Add the thyme leaves stripped from the stems or the dried herbs and stir over the heat to bring up the flavour. Spread the browned onion and garlic mixture on top of each fish portion.

**3** Melt the butter in a small saucepan and draw off the heat. Add the breadcrumbs and grated Parmesan and stir with a fork until the crumbs are butter coated. Spoon the Parmesan crumbs over the browned onion.

**4** Heat the oven to 190°C (375°F or gas no. 5). Set the dish in the heated oven and bake for 25–30 minutes until the fish flakes and the crumb topping is golden and crisp.

700 g (1½ lb) hake or haddock
  fillet
salt and freshly milled pepper
1 medium onion
2–3 cloves garlic
2 tablespoons olive oil
4 fresh thyme sprigs or ½
  teaspoon herbes de Provence
25 g (1 oz) butter
50 g (2 oz) fresh white
  breadcrumbs
25 g (1 oz) grated Parmesan
  cheese

**Serves 4**

Preparation time: 15 minutes
Cooking time: 20 minutes

# Teriyaki Salmon with Lentil and Onion Salad

4 salmon fillet portions, with
  skin on
2 tablespoons dark soy sauce
2 tablespoons soft brown
  sugar
juice 1 lemon
1 tablespoon grapeseed oil
freshly milled pepper
1 teaspoon grated fresh ginger

FOR THE LENTIL AND ONION
SALAD:

1 medium onion
2 cloves garlic
4 tablespoons olive oil
2 teaspoons caster sugar
2 tablespoons red wine
  vinegar
2 tablespoons dark soy sauce
salt and freshly milled pepper
1 x 432 g tin green lentils

**Serves 4**
Preparation time: 20 minutes,
  plus marinating time
Cooking time: 8–10 minutes

**1** Arrange the salmon portions in a single layer in a shallow dish. Mix together the soy sauce, soft brown sugar, lemon juice and grapeseed oil. Add a seasoning of pepper and the grated fresh ginger and mix again. Pour over the fish, turning to coat the pieces on both sides. Cover and leave to marinate for at least 2 hours.

**2** Meanwhile prepare the lentil and onion salad. Peel and thinly slice the onion and peel and crush the garlic. Heat 1 tablespoon of the olive oil in a large frying pan, add the onion and sprinkle with the sugar. Cook until the onion is soft and golden, stir frequently. Stir in the garlic. Add the remaining olive oil, the wine vinegar, the soy sauce and a seasoning of salt and pepper. Drain the lentils and tip into the pan. Stir gently and bring to the boil. Spoon into a serving bowl and leave to marinate for at least 1 hour or cover and refrigerate overnight.

**3** Heat the grill to medium hot and set the grill rack 7.5 cm (3 inches) from the heat source. Lift the salmon pieces from the marinade and place them skin side up in a flameproof baking dish. Set under the grill for 8–10 minutes, basting with the remaining marinade. Do not turn the fish pieces, cook them from one side only and allow the skin to brown and crinkle. Allow to cool and serve at room temperature with the lentil and onion salad.

# Salmon Parcels with Courgettes

**1** Arrange the salmon steaks in a single layer in a shallow dish. Mix together the oil, vinegar and pepper. Pour over the fish steaks, turning to coat them on both sides. Cover and marinate for 1 hour.
**2** Cut 4 squares of greaseproof paper, each one large enough to enclose a salmon steak. Brush each sheet on one side with oil. Trim the courgettes and slice. Heat the butter in a frying pan. Stir in the courgette slices and cook 3–4 minutes. Stir in the dill. Lift the salmon steaks from the marinade. Place one in the centre of each oiled sheet of greaseproof paper. Season with salt and top with the buttered courgettes. Draw opposite sides of the paper together over the fish and fold closed, turn folded ends underneath. Arrange fish parcels in one layer in a baking dish or on a baking tray.
**3** Heat the oven to 180°C (350°F or gas no. 4). Set the salmon parcels in the heated oven and bake for 15–20 minutes. Serve hot with extra melted butter flavoured with a slice of lemon on the side.

4 salmon steaks, about 2.5 cm
  (1 inch) thick
2 tablespoons grapeseed oil
2 tablespoons white wine
  vinegar
freshly milled pepper
225 g (8 oz) small courgettes
50 g (2 oz) butter
2–3 tablespoons chopped
  fresh dill
salt
50–75 g (2–3 oz) butter and
  1 lemon slice to serve

**Serves 4**
Preparation time: 20 minutes,
  plus marinating time
Cooking time: 15–20 minutes

# Peppered Salmon with Tomato and Avocado Vinaigrette

*In this delicious and pretty dish salmon takes the pepper flavour perfectly.*

**1** Cut out the stalk end, then scald the tomato in boiling water and peel away the skin. Cut in quarters and deseed, then dice the tomato flesh. Grate the lemon rind and squeeze the juice.

**2** Measure the extra virgin olive oil into a small bowl and add the lemon juice, grated rind, sugar and mustard. Stir to mix, season with salt and pepper and mix again. Trim the spring onions then chop all the white and some of the green stems. Add the spring onion and tomato to the vinaigrette and chill.

**3** Remove any skin on the reverse of the salmon fillets and brush the fish with 1 tablespoon of the olive oil and generously sprinkle with cracked pepper on both sides. Heat the remaining olive oil in a large frying pan, add the salmon pieces and cook for about 3 minutes on each side.

**4** While the salmon is cooking, halve the avocado, remove the stone and pull off the skin. Dice the flesh and add to the vinaigrette. Serve the peppered salmon fillets with the cool tomato and avocado vinaigrette.

1 beefsteak tomato
1 lemon
6 tablespoons extra virgin olive oil
1 teaspoon caster sugar
2 teaspoons Dijon mustard
salt and freshly milled pepper
1 bunch (6–8) spring onions
4 salmon fillet portions
3 tablespoons olive oil
2 teaspoons cracked black pepper
1 avocado

**Serves 4**

Preparation time: 15 minutes, plus chilling time
Cooking time: 6–8 minutes

# Baked Trout with Soy and Ginger

*Ask the fishmonger to gut the fish but leave them whole, he will offer to take the heads off the trout and that's up to you – I like them left on.*

**1** Heat the oven to 180°C (350° or gas no. 4). Using 1 tablespoon of the oil, rub the fish all over and lay them in an oiled baking dish. Trim the spring onions, then chop all the white and some of the green stems. Stack the slices of fresh ginger and cut lengthways and across to finely chop. Scatter the spring onions and ginger all over the fish.

**2** Cover the fish with oiled foil, set in the heated oven and bake for 25 minutes. Meanwhile measure the remaining oil, soy sauce and vinegar into a saucepan. Bring to a simmer, pour over the baked fish and serve.

4 tablespoons grapeseed or other light oil
2 rainbow trout
1 bunch (6–8) spring onions
2–3 thin slices pared fresh ginger
1 tablespoon soy sauce
2 tablespoons white wine vinegar

**Serves 2**

Preparation time: 20 minutes
Cooking time: 25 minutes

# Pickled Trout with Honey-Mustard Dressing

*A gravadlax sauce with fresh dill sprigs flavours these rolled pink trout fillets. Serve them with a fresh bean salad and thick slices of rye bread to mop up the juices.*

6 pink trout fillets
salt and freshly milled pepper
150 ml (¼ pint) white wine
vinegar
1 tablespoon green peppercorns
½ small onion, sliced in rings
25 g (1 oz) soft brown sugar

FOR THE DRESSING:

3 tablespoons Dijon mustard
1 tablespoon wholegrain
mustard
3 tablespoons clear honey
2 tablespoons white wine
vinegar
3 tablespoons grapeseed oil
fresh dill sprigs

**Serves 6**
Preparation time: 20 minutes
Cooking time: 35 minutes, plus
cooling time

**1** Heat the oven to 180°C (350°F or gas no. 4). Take each trout fillet and, with a sharp knife, remove the silvery skin and trim the fillet neatly. Turn the fillet skin side up, season and roll, starting at the tail end – the fleshy side will be on the outside.

**2** Arrange the rolled fillets in a baking dish, one in which they pack tightly and will remain rolled up. In a saucepan combine 150 ml (¼ pint) water, the vinegar, peppercorns, onion and brown sugar. Bring to a simmer, then pour the hot pickling mixture over the fillets – it should be sufficient to cover them. Cover the dish with a lid, set in the preheated oven and bake for 35 minutes. Let the fillets cool in the pickling mixture – the fish firms up and will take the flavour.

**3** Meanwhile, in a bowl combine the mustards, honey, vinegar and grapeseed oil for the dressing. To serve, drain the pickling marinade from the baking dish, garnish each fillet with a fresh dill sprig and pour over the honey-mustard dressing.

---

### NEW FISH ON THE BLOCK

Here are three of the best fish now available:

**Hoki:** Firm, skinless white fillets from New Zealand. Its cooking characteristics are comparable with cod, so use in similar recipes.

**Snapper:** A well-flavoured red, grey or pink fish, suited to dishes with robust flavours. Cook whole.

**St Peter's fish (or tilapia):** A silver or red fresh-water fish (right). Firm white flesh, excellent marinated or rubbed with spices and baked or steamed.

# Grilled Sea Trout

**1** With a sharp knife, slash through the thickest part of the fish 3 or 4 times on each side to aid cooking and make serving easier. Melt 50 g (2 oz) of the butter in a saucepan.

**2** Heat the grill to moderately hot. Place the fish on the grill rack and brush lavishly with about half of the melted butter. Place the fish under the grill and cook for 10 minutes – the skin will char and crisp. Carefully turn over the fish and brush the remaining melted butter on the second side. Replace under the grill for 8 minutes (the second side requires less cooking time).

**3** Transfer the fish to a warm platter. Cut along the back and lift the flesh off the bone – the deep cuts will encourage portions to come away in neat pieces. Melt the remaining butter and add a seasoning of salt and pepper and the lemon juice. Serve the fish hot with the butter mixture.

1 sea trout or small salmon, about 1.1–1.5 kg (2½–3 lb)
100 g (4 oz) butter
salt and freshly milled pepper
juice ½ lemon

**Serves 6**
Preparation time: 10 minutes
Cooking time: 20 minutes

# Sea Bass Fillets with Stir-Fried Leeks, Soy and Ginger

**1** Heat the oven to 220°C (425°F or gas no. 7). Wash and trim the leeks cutting the green stalk to within 5 cm (2 inches) of the white stem. Slice leeks finely. Trim the spring onions, then chop all the white and some of the green stems. Pare and coarsely grate the fresh ginger. Combine the vinegar and soy sauce.

**2** Cut each sea bass fillet in two, lightly coat with olive oil and a seasoning of salt and pepper. Arrange them on a roasting tray, skin side up. Set in the hot oven and roast for 10 minutes, or until done.

**3** Meanwhile set a wok or large 25 cm (10 inch) frying pan over a moderate heat. Add the grapeseed oil and when the oil is hot, add the spring onions and ginger and stir-fry for 1 minute to flavour the oil. Add the leeks and stir-fry for 2–3 minutes until the leeks are wilted and shiny. Add the vinegar and soy sauce mixture, stir and draw off the heat.

**4** Spoon the stir-fried leeks onto 4 heated plates. Arrange the sea bass fillets on top and serve.

700 g (2 lb) leeks
1 bunch (6–8) spring onions
2.5 cm (1 inch) fresh ginger
3 tablespoons cider or wine vinegar
1 tablespoon soy sauce
2 sea bass, each about 700 g (1½ lb), filleted
olive oil
salt and freshly milled pepper
2 tablespoons grapeseed or other light oil

**Serves 4**
Preparation time: 15 minutes
Cooking time: 12–15 minutes

# Rolled Fillets with Prawns and Parmesan Sauce

**1** Using a sharp kitchen knife, skin the plaice fillets, then separate each piece into 2 narrow fillets to make 12 pieces of fish altogether. Season with salt and freshly milled pepper. Roll up each piece of fish with the prawns inside and secure with a cocktail stick. Arrange the rolled fillets in a single layer in a buttered 1.1 litre (2 pint) baking dish and sprinkle over the lemon juice.

**2** Heat the oven to 180°C (350°F or gas no. 4). Cover the fish with buttered kitchen foil, set in the heated oven and bake for 15–20 minutes or until the plaice is white and flakes to the touch.

**3** Meanwhile, melt the butter in a saucepan, stir in the flour and cook for 1 minute. Gradually stir in the milk, beating well to make a smooth sauce. Bring to a simmer and cook gently for 1–2 minutes. Draw off the heat and season with salt and freshly milled pepper and a little nutmeg. Add the Parmesan and stir until melted.

**4** Heat the grill to hot and set the grill rack about 7.5 cm (3 inches) from the heat source. Strain any liquid from the cooked fish into the sauce and stir in the blended egg yolk and single cream. Spoon the sauce over the fish fillets.

**5** Place the dish under the heated grill until the sauce is bubbling and patches of brown appear – this looks appetising. Sprinkle with grated Parmesan and return the dish to the grill for a moment more to brown the cheese. Remove the cocktail sticks and serve.

6 filleted plaice halves, each
   about 225 g (8 oz) each
salt and freshly milled pepper
225 g (8 oz) cooked and
   peeled prawns
2 tablespoons lemon juice
25 g (1 oz) butter
25 g (1 oz) flour
300 ml (½ pint) milk
grated nutmeg
25 g (1 oz) Parmesan cheese
1 egg yolk
2 tablespoons single cream
Parmesan cheese for
   sprinkling

**Serves 6**
Preparation time: 25 minutes
Cooking time: 25–30 minutes

---

### Katie's Tip
...............................
A white sauce tends to form a skin if it sits waiting to be used. My trick is to stir in all but one third of the liquid over the heat, then float a film of the remaining liquid over the top of the sauce and keep it warm over a low heat. Stir only when ready to use.

# Vegetables

The flavour and variety of vegetables provide endless opportunities for imaginative recipes. Try to cook vegetables on a seasonal basis – offer braised cabbage, mixed roast vegetables and sweet potatoes for winter menus, while summer demands delicious fresh peas and beans or quick stir-fries. Accompaniments to vegetables are here too.

*Mushroom Crêpes*

# Mushroom Crêpes

12 prepared crêpes (recipe
  below)
700 g (1½ lb) open cup
  mushrooms
1 medium onion
2–3 cloves garlic
50 g (2 oz) butter
1 tablespoon soy sauce
½ teaspoon dried thyme
salt and freshly milled pepper
225 g (8 oz) curd cheese

**Serves 6**
Preparation time: 45 minutes,
  plus cooling time
Cooking time: 20–30 minutes

**1** Have the crêpes ready made (set below). Set aside six mushrooms. Remove the stalks from the remainder and discard. Chop the mushrooms finely with a kitchen knife. Peel and finely chop the onion; peel and crush the garlic.

**2** Melt 25 g (1 oz) butter in a frying pan, add the onion and soften – about 5 minutes. Add the garlic and chopped mushrooms and continue to cook gently, uncovered, until the mushrooms are soft and any liquid has evaporated – about 20 minutes. They will be quite dark in colour. Stir in the soy sauce, thyme and a seasoning of salt and pepper. Draw off the heat and cool.

**3** Turn the curd cheese into a mixing bowl. Add the mushroom mixture and mash with fork. Or, buzz in a food processor for a smoother mixture. Separate the crêpes and place a spoonful of the mushroom filling on one half of each. Fold over the other half to make half-moon shapes.

**4** Melt the remaining butter and use a little of it to brush round the inside of a 1.1 litre (2 pint) shallow baking dish. Tuck the filled crêpes in the baking dish, slightly overlapping.

**5** Heat the oven to 180°C (350°F or gas no. 4). Cover the pancakes with kitchen foil, set in the heated oven and bake for 20–30 minutes until heated through. Meanwhile, thickly slice the reserved mushrooms and sauté in the rest of the melted butter. Spoon over as the mushroom pancakes are served.

**Basic crêpe recipe:** Sift 100g (4 oz) plain flour and a pinch of salt into a mixing bowl. Make a well in the centre. Break 1 egg and 1 egg yolk into the well and add 150 ml (¼ pint) milk. Using a wooden spoon, stir from the centre gradually drawing in the flour from around the sides of the bowl. Beat to a thick batter. Stir in a further 150 ml (¼ pint) milk and 1 tablespoon melted butter or oil. Pour the batter into a jug.

Heat a 15 cm (6 inch) crêpe or omelette pan and grease lightly. Pour in a very thin layer of batter (about 2 tablespoons) and tip the pan to spread evenly over the base. When browned on the underside, loosen the crêpe, turn it over and cook the second side. Slide the crêpe on to absorbent kitchen paper and start making the next one.

# Potato Galette

**1** Peel the potatoes and slice them thinly, a mandoline vegetable slicer or your food processor will do the best job.

**2** Heat the oven to 200°C (400°F or gas no. 6). Using 15 g (½ oz) of the butter, well grease the inside of a 20 cm (8 inch) sponge cake tin. Arrange neat layers of the potato slices to fill the tin, add flakes of the remaining butter and a seasoning of salt and milled pepper to the layers as you arrange them. Cover with a square of buttered foil. Set the galette in the heated oven and bake for 45 minutes to 1 hour or until the potatoes are tender – test with a knife tip. Remove the foil covering.

**3** Place a serving plate over the tin, then invert both the plate and the potato layers. Lift the tin away. Place the potato galette under a hot grill for a few minutes to brown the surface. Cut into slices and serve hot.

900 g (2 lb) maincrop
   potatoes
40 g (1½ oz) butter
salt and freshly milled pepper

**Serves 4**
Preparation time: 20 minutes
Cooking time: 45 minutes–1 hour

# Leek and Potato Gratin

*Serve hot with your favourite cold sliced meat – ham or turkey are especially good.*

**1** Trim and cut the leeks across in 1 cm (½ inch) slices. Pare and cut the potatoes into 1 cm (½ inch) dice. Pour boiling water over the leeks to blanch them, then drain. Cover the potatoes with cold water, bring to a simmer and cook for 2 minutes, then drain.

**2** In a large mixing bowl, combine the cream, eggs, a seasoning of salt, pepper and grated nutmeg and mix well. Grate the smoked Cheddar and add half to the bowl. Turn the leeks and potatoes into the cream mixture and stir to mix.

**3** Heat the oven to 180°C (350°F or gas no. 4). Lightly oil a 1.1 litre (2 pint) shallow baking dish and heat it in the oven for 5 minutes. Remove from the oven, pour in the leek and potato mixture and spread evenly. Top with the remaining grated Cheddar cheese. Place in the oven and bake for 40 minutes or until puffed and golden. Serve at once.

2 leeks
700 g (1½ lb) baking potatoes
150 ml (¼ pint) double cream
2 eggs
salt and freshly milled pepper
grated nutmeg
100 g (4 oz) smoked Cheddar
   cheese

**Serves 6**
Preparation time: 30 minutes
Cooking time: 40 minutes

# Grilled Fennel with Marinated Feta Cheese

3–4 bulbs fennel
olive oil for grilling
6 tablespoons virgin olive oil
2 tablespoons lemon juice
2–3 fresh oregano sprigs
salt and freshly milled pepper
150 g (5 oz) feta cheese
100 g (4 oz) Italian olives

**Serves 6**

Preparation time: 25 minutes,
  plus marinating time
Cooking time: 8–10 minutes

**1** Snip the feathery bits from the fennel and discard, keeping the bulbs whole without any further trimming. Add the bulbs to a saucepan of boiling salted water, return to a simmer and blanch for 5 minutes. Drain and cool under the cold tap, then dry.

**2** Slice each bulb in half lengthways, then cut the halves into quarters or thirds to make wedges – by cutting lengthways each time the layers of the fennel stay intact.

**3** Heat the grill to hot and set the grill rack 7.5 cm (3 inches) from the heat source. Arrange the fennel pieces on a baking tray and brush with olive oil. Grill, turning them once or twice, brushing with oil, until tinged brown, soft and sweet-flavoured – about 8 minutes. Arrange on a serving dish.

**4** Combine the olive oil, lemon juice, coarsely chopped oregano and a seasoning of salt and pepper in a bowl for the dressing. Slice or break the feta cheese into pieces, add to the dressing and marinate until serving time. Then spoon feta cheese and dressing over the salad. Add the olives and serve.

# Braised Red Cabbage with Orange

*Red cabbage is one of the few vegetables that can be cooked ahead and reheated, which will make it taste even better.*

1 small or ½ large red cabbage
1 medium onion
25 g (1 oz) butter
grated rind and juice 1 orange
2 tablespoons red wine
  vinegar
50 g (2 oz) caster sugar
50 g (2 oz) seedless raisins
salt and freshly milled pepper

**Serves 6**

Preparation time: 20 minutes
Cooking time: 1½ hours

**1** Remove any damaged outer leaves and cut the red cabbage in quarters. Slice away the white core and shred the cabbage across the leaves. Peel and finely chop the onion.

**2** Melt the butter in a large saucepan. Add the chopped onion and fry gently to soften. Add the red cabbage and the grated orange rind. Squeeze the orange juice and make up to 150 ml (¼ pint) with water. Add to the saucepan along with the vinegar, sugar, raisins and a seasoning of salt and milled pepper.

**3** Cover with the pan lid and bring to a simmer. Lower the heat and cook gently for about 1½ hours. Stir or shake the pan occasionally. When cooked and ready to serve, the red cabbage will be soft and tender and the liquid will have evaporated.

# Peas in the French Style

**1** Trim the roots and green stems from the spring onions, leaving the bulbs whole. Remove coarse outer leaves from the lettuce, then cut the firm heart lengthways into quarters or across in shreds.
**2** Melt 40 g (1½ oz) of the butter in a medium saucepan. Add the lettuce, spring onion bulbs, a seasoning of salt and freshly milled pepper, the sugar, the peas and 2 tablespoons cold water.
**3** Cover with the pan lid and place over a medium heat. After 3–4 minutes when the ingredients are bubbling, reduce the heat to the lowest setting and cook for 20 minutes – shake the pan occasionally without removing the lid. Check the seasoning, stir in the rest of the butter, the chopped parsley or chervil and serve the contents of the pan.

1 bunch (6–8) spring onions
1 small cos or little gem
  lettuce
50 g (2 oz) butter
salt and freshly milled pepper
1 level teaspoon caster sugar
500 g (18 oz) shelled peas
1 tablespoon chopped fresh
  parsley or chervil

**Serves 4–6**
Preparation time: 10 minutes
Cooking time: 20–25 minutes

# Flageolet Beans with Olive Oil, Garlic and Herbs

**1** Drain the soaked flageolet beans and cover them with fresh cold water in a saucepan. Add the bay leaves. Bring to the boil for 10 minutes, then lower the heat and simmer gently for 1 hour or until tender, then drain.
**2** Peel and crush the garlic. Rinse and dry the cooking pan and set back over the heat with the olive oil and the garlic. Heat for a moment to allow the oil to take the flavour of the garlic, but do not let the garlic brown. Draw off the heat and then add the hot cooked flageolets.
**3** Toss the contents of the pan, add a good seasoning of salt and freshly milled pepper and the chopped herbs and toss again. Serve hot – with roast lamb or chicken.

250 g (9 oz) flageolet beans,
  soaked overnight
2 bay leaves
3–4 cloves garlic
3 tablespoons olive oil
salt and freshly milled pepper
2 tablespoons chopped fresh
  parsley or tarragon

**Serves 4**
Preparation time: 10 minutes,
  plus soaking time
Cooking time: 1¼ hours

# Cheese and Bacon Cauliflower

1 large cauliflower
1 medium onion
6 lean bacon rashers
50 g (2 oz) butter
40 g (1½ oz) plain flour
300 ml (½ pint) milk
salt and freshly milled pepper
grated nutmeg
100 g (4 oz) grated mature
  Cheddar cheese

FOR THE CRUMB TOPPING:

2 tablespoons grated
  Parmesan cheese
50 g (2 oz) fresh white
  breadcrumbs
25 g (1 oz) melted butter
hot dry toast to serve

**Serves 3**
Preparation time: 25 minutes
Cooking time: 15–20 minutes

**1** Trim the cauliflower, cutting it into medium-sized florets. Cook the florets in a pan of boiling salted water until just tender – about 8–10 minutes. Drain, reserving 150 ml (¼ pint) of the water for the sauce. Arrange the cauliflower in a buttered 1.4 litre (2½ pint) baking dish.

**2** Peel and finely chop the onion. Trim the bacon rashers then snip them into pieces. Put the onion and the bacon in a dry frying pan and sauté together until the bacon fat runs and the onion has softened. Sprinkle the bacon and onion over the cauliflower.

**3** Melt the butter in a medium saucepan, stir in the flour and cook for 1 minute. Stir in first the reserved cauliflower water and then the milk, beating well all the time to get a smooth sauce. Bring to a simmer and cook for 2–3 minutes. Add a seasoning of salt and freshly milled pepper and a grating of nutmeg. Off the heat, stir in the grated cheese, then pour the sauce over the cauliflower.

**4** Heat the oven to 190°C (375°F or gas no. 5). Meanwhile, make the crumb topping: combine the grated Parmesan and breadcrumbs. Add the melted butter and fork through to moisten the crumbs. Sprinkle over the cauliflower. Set in the preheated oven for 15–20 minutes until it's bubbling and the top is crispy and golden. Serve with slices of hot dry toast.

# Cauliflower with a Crumb Topping

50 g (2 oz) butter
75 g (3 oz) fresh white
  breadcrumbs
1 teaspoon grated lemon rind
salt and freshly milled pepper
2 tablespoons chopped fresh
  parsley
1 medium cauliflower

**Serves 4**
Preparation time: 20 minutes
Cooking time: 15 minutes

**1** Start with the crumb topping. Melt the butter in a frying pan, add the breadcrumbs and fry, stirring until the crumbs are crisp and golden – about 5–6 minutes. Draw the pan off the heat and add the grated lemon rind, a seasoning of salt and milled pepper and the chopped parsley. Stir to mix and reserve.

**2** Separate the cauliflower into large florets. Add to boiling salted water and cook until the stems are just tender, about 8–10 minutes then drain. Arrange the florets in a buttered heatproof serving dish.

**3** Spoon the crumb topping over the cauliflower and serve. If you have prepared the crumb mixture ahead, put the crumb-topped cauliflower into an oven 160°C (325°F or gas no. 3) for 15 minutes to crisp up.

# Carrots with Butter and Brown Sugar

700 g (1½ lb) carrots
2 tablespoons soft brown
  sugar
25 g (1 oz) butter
salt and freshly milled pepper
½ teaspoon cracked pepper

**Serves 6**
Preparation time: 10 minutes
Cooking time: 30–40 minutes

**1** Heat the oven to 180°C (350°F or gas no. 4). Trim the carrots, pare and then cut lengthways and across in chunky sticks. Cover the carrots with cold salted water, bring to the boil and simmer for 10 minutes, then drain.

**2** Arrange the hot carrots in a buttered casserole in layers with the sugar, the butter in flakes and a seasoning of salt and milled pepper. Add 2 tablespoons cold water. Cover and cook for a further 20–30 minutes. Sprinkle with cracked pepper (sometimes called steak pepper) and serve.

# Sweet Potatoes with Brown Sugar and Orange

900 g (2 lb) sweet potatoes
2 tablespoons soft brown
  sugar
grated rind 1 orange
25 g (1 oz) butter

**Serves 4**
Preparation time: 10 minutes
Cooking time: 40–45 minutes

**1** Scrub the potatoes, but don't peel and, if very large, cut into big chunks. Bring to the boil in salted water to cover and simmer for 20–30 minutes until fork tender, then drain. Cool for 5 minutes, peel off the skins and slice thickly.

**2** Heat the oven to 180°C (350°F or gas no. 4). Layer the potatoes in a 1.7 litre (3 pint) buttered baking dish, sprinkling them with the soft brown sugar, orange rind and the butter, cut in flakes.

**3** Set in the oven and bake for 20–25 minutes, until the potatoes are hot and glazed.

---

### Katie's Tip

Sweet potatoes are always cooked in their jackets. If peeled before cooking, they discolour very quickly. I often cut large ones to fit them in my saucepan. If not cooked immediately, drop them into a bowl of cold salted water and cook them as soon after as you can.

---

# Puy Lentils with Bacon

**1** Rinse the lentils (no need to soak), cover with fresh cold water and bring to the boil, lower the heat and simmer for 30 minutes until tender, then drain. Peel and slice the onion and peel and crush the garlic.

**2** Heat the oil in a frying pan. Add the sliced onion and bacon lardons. Stir and fry the mixture until the onion is softened and begins to brown and the bacon pieces are frizzled – about 10 minutes. Stir in the garlic and the fresh thyme.

**3** Add the drained lentils, a seasoning of salt and freshly milled pepper and the vinegar. Taste for seasoning. Sprinkle with chopped parsley and serve – with roasted duck or grilled chicken.

250 g (9 oz) Puy lentils
1 medium onion
2 cloves garlic
1 tablespoon olive oil
100 g (4 oz) bacon lardons
1 tablespoon crumbled fresh
   thyme leaves
salt and freshly milled pepper
1 tablespoon balsamic or red
   wine vinegar
2 tablespoons chopped fresh
   parsley

**Serves 4**
Preparation time: 15 minutes
Cooking time: 45 minutes

# Oven-Roasted Tomatoes

*These have an intense tomato flavour; perch them on crostini and serve with drinks, add to salads or to hot pasta with grated Parmesan cheese.*

**1** Heat the oven to 180°C (350°F or gas no. 4). With a small vegetable knife cut out and discard the stalk end of each tomato. Then cut the tomatoes in half lengthways. Lightly oil a roasting tin. Arrange the tomatoes in the roasting tin, cut surface upwards. Season with salt and freshly milled pepper and the caster sugar and sprinkle with the dried herbs.

**2** Drizzle about 2 tablespoons of olive oil over the tomatoes, place in the preheated oven and bake for 40–45 minutes. About halfway through the cooking time, stab the tomatoes with the prongs of a fork to encourage the juices to run. When roasted the tomatoes will have collapsed and shrivelled and will have a concentrated tomato flavour. Remove from the heat and cool to room temperature.

450–700 g (1–1½ lb) plum
   tomatoes
salt and freshly milled pepper
1 teaspoon caster sugar
1 teaspoon dried oregano or
   herbes de Provence
2 tablespoons olive oil

**Serves 4–6**
Preparation time: 20 minutes
Cooking time: 40–45 minutes

# Creamed Purée of Spinach

900 g (2 lb) fresh spinach
25 g (1 oz) butter
2 tablespoons plain flour
300 ml (½ pint) milk
salt and freshly milled pepper
3 eggs
2 tablespoons double cream
grated nutmeg

**Serves 6**
Preparation time: 30 minutes
Cooking time: 1 hour

**1** Tear away the coarse stems and wash the spinach in cold water. Reserve about 6 of the best large leaves. Lift the rest of the leaves from the water and pack into a saucepan. Cover with the pan lid and cook over a moderate heat until the spinach is soft – water clinging to the leaves will provide sufficient liquid. Drain well pressing out excess water. Purée the spinach in a food processor or pass through a vegetable mouli.

**2** Meanwhile prepare a sauce by melting the butter in a saucepan over a low heat. Stir in the flour and cook for 1 minute. Gradually beat in the milk, stirring well to get a smooth sauce. Bring to a simmer, season with salt and milled pepper and cook 2–3 minutes. Draw off the heat. Stir in the spinach purée, eggs, cream and a grating of nutmeg.

**3** Put the reserved spinach leaves in a colander and pour through boiling water from the kettle to soften them. Press out excess water and use the leaves to line a buttered 15 cm (6 inch) soufflé dish or 750 ml (1¼ pint) pudding basin allowing the leaves to overhang the sides. Pour in the creamed spinach mixture and turn the overlapping spinach leaves in over the filling. Cover with buttered greaseproof paper or buttered foil. Cool and chill until serving time.

**4** Heat the oven to 160°C (325°F or gas no. 3). Set the dish of creamed spinach in a large roasting tin. Pour in boiling water from the kettle to 2.5 cm (1 inch) in depth. Set in the centre of the preheated oven and bake for 1 hour. Let cool 5 minutes, then turn out and serve.

---

### Katie's Tip

Nutmeg is one of my favourite spices. My whole nutmegs are so highly prized that I keep them in a small silver-topped jar and use them up at a terrific rate. There is no need for a special gadget; the small teeth on a cheese grater will grind them very finely – just grate directly into any spinach, cheese or meat recipe and to flavour white sauce.

# Hot Vegetable Platter

*Group vegetables together on one large platter to make a feature of them. Your choice of vegetables can be whatever suits your menu and include as few or as many as you can reasonably cook.*

**1** Trim the stalk ends from the mangetout and the green beans but leave on the pretty tails. Separate the broccoli into small florets. Cut back the outer leaves on the cauliflower but leave the tiny inner green ones. Then cut the cauliflower head into thirds or quarters depending on the size. Scrub the new potatoes leaving on the skins. Steam the new potatoes (10 minutes). In a pan of boiling salted water, start with the cauliflower (8 minutes), lift from the pan with a slotted spoon. Keep the cooked vegetables covered, draining in a colander or sieve. Now add the broccoli florets to the boiling water (5 minutes). In a frying pan of simmering water start with the green beans (6 minutes), lift from the pan with a slotted spoon, then add the mangetout (3 minutes).

**2** Meanwhile melt the butter. Add a thinly pared piece of lemon rind, freshly milled pepper and the chopped herbs. Pour into a serving bowl. Stir the mayonnaise and mix in a tablespoon of boiling water to thin it down for a better sauce consistency and turn into a serving bowl. Arrange the vegetables on a hot platter and serve the sauces separately with lemon wedges and sea salt.

225 g (8 oz) mangetout
225 g (8 oz) green beans
350 g (12 oz) broccoli
1 cauliflower
450 g (1 lb) new potatoes
75 g (3 oz) butter
pared lemon rind
freshly milled pepper
2 tablespoons chopped fresh
  parsley, tarragon or chives
300 ml (½ pint) mayonnaise
lemons and sea salt to serve

**Serves 4–6**
Preparation time: 15–20 minutes
Cooking time: 30–35 minutes

---

### Katie's Tip

Simmering vegetables get a flavour boost if you omit the salt and crumble in a vegetable stock cube instead.

# Mixed Vegetable Stir-Fry

**1** Pare the carrots, then cut lengthways into thin matchstick strips. Top and tail the mangetout. Trim and blanch the sweetcorn in boiling water for 3 minutes to tenderise, then drain. Rinse and dry the bean sprouts. Trim the spring onions, then finely shred the white and pale green stems on the diagonal. Pare the fresh ginger and coarsely grate.

**2** Heat the oil in a wok (or frying pan), add the cashew nuts and stir-fry to brown them. Transfer them to a plate. Add the spring onion and grated ginger to the hot oil and stir-fry for 30 seconds.

**3** Add the carrot sticks and sweetcorn and stir-fry for 3 minutes. Add the mangetout and bean sprouts and stir-fry for a further 2 minutes. Return the cashew nuts to the pan, sprinkle with sesame oil and serve. Stir-fried vegetables can make a good side dish with grilled meats.

100 g (4 oz) young carrots
100 g (4 oz) mangetout
100 g (4 oz) whole baby
  sweetcorn
100 g (4 oz) bean sprouts
1 bunch (6–8) spring onions
2.5 cm (1 inch) fresh ginger
2 tablespoons grapeseed oil
2 tablespoons cashew nuts
sesame oil for sprinkling

**Serves 2**
Preparation time: 15 minutes
Cooking time: 8 minutes

---

### Katie's Tip
.................................
A good all-purpose frying pan of at least 25 cm (10 inch) diameter (so there's plenty of room) is a perfectly good pan for stir-frying. And if it's non-stick, so much the better. Woks are deeper than frying pans. The traditional style with a rounded base is fine on a gas hob, but for electric cookers choose one with a flat bottom that will sit steady and absorb the heat evenly. Other essentials are a stir-fry spatula and a slotted (perforated) spoon for lifting food temporarily from the pan but leaving the oil behind.

# Fried Chicory

*Chicory has a marvellous bitter flavour and it tastes absolutely wonderful with pheasant. I had never tasted this particular vegetable hot until I was shown how to prepare it this way – the recipe comes from Belgium. Fried chicory does need last minute attention but you can get it half prepared ahead.*

6 heads chicory
2–3 tablespoons seasoned
  flour
50 g (2 oz) butter

**Serves 6**
Preparation time: 10 minutes
Cooking time: 15 minutes

**1** Choose heads of chicory that are firm and plump and ones with the palest yellow tinges to the leaves – green edges mean the chicory has been exposed to the light and will have a stronger flavour. Remove any outer damaged leaves and trim the stalk end. Add the whole heads to a saucepan of boiling salted water and simmer until barely tender – about 10 minutes. Drain very thoroughly and leave until cold.

**2** Place the sifted seasoned flour on a plate. Roll each head of chicory in the flour and set aside for the final stages of cooking.

**3** Melt the butter in a roomy frying pan and when hot and foaming add the floured chicory. Fry fairly quickly, turning the heads once or twice, until the chicory is golden brown and crisp, then serve at once.

---

## SPUDS YOU'LL LIKE

**Mash:** Press peeled and cooked potatoes through a vegetable mouli, season, add warmed milk and beat until smooth. Top with browned, butter-fried onion.

**Roast wedges:** Scrub potatoes and cut lengthways into wedges. Brush out surfaces with olive oil, sprinkle with sea salt and paprika. Roast until tender and crisp – about 40 minutes.

**Crunchy skins:** Bake potatoes, then cut in half. Scoop out the centres leaving a thin layer of potato. Cut skins in quarters. Brush with olive oil, sprinkle with paprika. Return to the oven until golden and crisp. Nice with soured cream and chive dip.

# Julienne of Celery and Potato

*Take this straight from the oven to the table. Delicious served with venison or game casseroles.*

**1** Peel and finely chop the onion. Separate the celery into stalks. Trim, then cut the celery stalks lengthways and across into 5 cm (2 inch) thick sticks. Peel the potatoes, then slice. Stack the potato slices and cut lengthways into sticks the same size as the celery.

**2** Heat the oven to 180°C (350°F or gas no. 4). Using 15 g (½ oz) of the butter, grease the inside of a 1.1 litre (2 pint) baking dish. Melt the remaining butter and oil in a large frying pan. Add the onion and soften gently for 3–4 minutes. Then add the celery sticks and turn in the hot butter and onion for 2–3 minutes. Add the potato sticks and turn the mixture again. Season well with salt and pepper and toss the vegetables to mix in the seasoning.

**3** Transfer the whole lot to the baking dish and cover with a lid or buttered foil. Set in the preheated oven and bake for about 45 minutes – test the vegetables for tenderness with a knife tip. Do not stir the vegetable mixture during or after cooking: this will cause the potatoes to break up. Serve from the baking dish.

1 medium onion
1 head celery
700 g (1½ lb) maincrop
   potatoes
40 g (1½ oz) butter
3 tablespoons olive oil
salt and freshly milled pepper

**Serves 6**
Preparation time: 20 minutes
Cooking time: 45 minutes

# Mixed Roast Winter Vegetables

**1** Pare the carrots and cut diagonally into thick slices. Pare the parsnips and potatoes and cut into 2.5 cm (1 inch) chunks. Pare the butternut squash, halve and remove seeds and cut squash in pieces. Peel the onions or shallots and leave them whole. It's important that the vegetable pieces are not too large and all about the same size so they cook evenly.

**2** Heat the oven to 190°C (375°F or gas no. 5). Place a large roasting tin in the oven as it heats up. Remove the hot tin from the oven and add 2 tablespoons of the olive oil. Add the prepared vegetables and drizzle over the remaining olive oil.

**3** Set in the heated oven and roast for 45 minutes, turning the vegetables once or twice to brown them. Towards the end of the cooking time you can add chopped fresh thyme leaves. Then before serving, sprinkle with sea salt and chopped parsley if you prefer it to thyme – the colour of parsley makes the vegetables look good.

3 medium carrots
2 parsnips
4 maincrop potatoes
1 butternut squash
6–8 small onions or shallots
4–6 tablespoons olive oil
sea salt
1 tablespoon chopped fresh
   thyme or parsley

**Serves 4–6**
Preparation time: 15 minutes
Cooking time: 45 minutes

# Salads

Salads are a visual feast of bright colours and pretty shapes. Contrasting colours and textures with well-flavoured dressings are what make a good recipe. Here you will find some salads to serve as side dishes and others substantial enough to weigh in as main dishes for hot summer days.

*New Potato, Bacon and Egg Salad*

# New Potato, Bacon and Egg Salad

450 g (1 lb) new potatoes

100 g (4 oz) green beans

225 g (8 oz) streaky bacon
  rashers

3 eggs

1 bunch (6–8) spring onions

2 tablespoons finely chopped
  fresh parsley and chives

FOR THE MUSTARD
DRESSING:

1 teaspoon Dijon mustard

3 tablespoons white wine
  vinegar

1 tablespoon caster sugar

100 ml (4 fl oz) olive oil

salt and freshly milled pepper

**Serves 4**

Preparation time: 10 minutes

Cooking time: 25–30 minutes

**1** For the mustard dressing, combine the Dijon mustard, white wine vinegar, caster sugar, olive oil and seasoning in a mixing bowl.

**2** Scrub the potatoes, leaving on the skins. Add to a saucepan of boiling water and cook for 10–15 minutes or until tender, then drain. Slice the hot potatoes thickly. Put them in a mixing bowl, with the mustard dressing and allow to cool.

**3** Top and tail the beans. Add to boiling salted water, or steam until tender. Allow to cool. Trim the bacon rashers and snip into large pieces. Put in a dry frying pan and sauté until crisp.

**4** Add the eggs to boiling salted water and simmer for 8 minutes. Drain and cover with cold water until cool, then shell. Trim and finely chop the spring onions.

**5** Add the beans, spring onions, chopped herbs and bacon to the potatoes. Spoon into a serving dish. Cut the eggs in quarters and add to the salad. Drizzle over any dressing left in the mixing bowl and serve.

---

### TAKE A LEAF

**Rocket:** Smooth, indented, dark tender leaves with a peppery flavour.

**Spinach:** Only small leaf spinach is tender enough to use in salads; pull away the stalks.

**Lamb's lettuce:** Clusters of tiny leaves with a nutty taste.

**Cress:** Adds a pretty contrast when scissor-snipped into other green leaves.

**Frisée:** Coarse and bitter, the outer leaves are stronger-flavoured than the middle ones. Use in small amounts.

**Radicchio:** The purple leaves add colour. A small head goes a long way.

**Dandelion:** Use young leaves – pick before flowers bloom.

**Watercress:** The dark green leaves and stalks will open up salad mixtures.

**Oak leaf lettuce:** Ragged leaves with purple shading.

# New Potato Salad with Salami, Green Beans and Basil

**1** Rinse the potatoes, add to boiling salted water, simmer until just tender. Drain and turn the potatoes onto a dry tea cloth (to absorb the moisture) then cut the potatoes into halves. Meanwhile trim and cut the beans in half. Cook the beans in boiling salted water until just tender – about 5 minutes, then drain.
**2** In a mixing bowl combine the olive oil, lemon juice and pesto. Peel and crush the garlic and add. Stir to make a dressing. Turn the warm potatoes into the bowl, season with salt and freshly milled pepper and turn in the dressing. Leave for 1 hour to take the flavour.
**3** Stack the salami slices and cut across 2 or 3 times to make strips, separate the pieces and add to the salad along with the cooked beans and the olives. Toss the mixture and turn onto a serving platter. Scatter with basil leaves.

500 g (18 oz) new potatoes
175 g (6 oz) French beans
4 tablespoons olive oil
2 tablespoons lemon juice
2–3 tablespoons pesto
1 clove garlic
salt and freshly milled pepper
100 g (4 oz) Italian salami
12 pitted black olives
fresh basil leaves to garnish

**Serves 4**

Preparation time: 15 minutes,
    plus marinating time
Cooking time: 15 minutes

# New Potatoes, Prawns and Cucumber in Dill Dressing

**1** Rinse the new potatoes and leave skins on. Add to boiling salted water and cook for 12 minutes, or until tender, then drain. Roll the potatoes on a clean tea cloth (to absorb the moisture), then slice thickly into a mixing bowl.
**2** Add the dressing while the potatoes are still warm and toss. Trim the spring onions, then chop all the white and some of the green stems. Add to the potatoes along with 1 tablespoon of the chopped dill. Leave until cold.
**3** Meanwhile combine the mayonnaise, yoghurt, mustard and a seasoning of salt and pepper. Slice the dill pickled cucumbers lengthways and across into dice. Add the diced cucumber and prawns to the mayonnaise mixture and blend. Let the salad stand until serving time.
**4** Then combine the two mixtures, turn onto a serving platter and sprinkle with the remaining chopped dill.

500 g (18 oz) new potatoes
2 tablespoons Fresh Herb
    Dressing (see page 158)
1 bunch (6–8) spring onions
2 tablespoons chopped fresh
    dill
2 tablespoons mayonnaise
2 tablespoons natural yoghurt
½ teaspoon Dijon mustard
salt and freshly milled pepper
4 dill pickled cucumbers
250 g (9 oz) cooked and
    peeled tiger prawns

**Serves 4**

Preparation time: 20 minutes,
    plus cooling time
Cooking time: 12 minutes

# Cos Lettuce Salad with Caesar Dressing

**1** Cut the crusts off the bread slices and discard or, if using a small baguette cut into 1 cm (½ inch) slices. Then cut the bread slices into small cubes. Heat the vegetable oil in a frying pan. Add the bread cubes and fry 1–2 minutes, stirring until they are crisp and brown. Lift out and drain on absorbent kitchen paper.

**2** Separate the lettuce leaves, wash and dry thoroughly. Tear larger leaves into 2–3 pieces, leave small leaves whole. Enclose lettuce in a polythene bag and refrigerate until serving time. Bring eggs to the boil from cold and cook for 6 minutes to hard boil, then plunge into cold water to arrest cooking and cool.

**3** For the dressing, crack the egg into a blender or food processor bowl. Add the lemon juice, a seasoning of salt and freshly milled pepper and the Worcestershire sauce. Peel and crush the garlic and add along with the Parmesan cheese. Cover and buzz to blend. Then, with the motor running, slowly pour in the oil until the dressing is thick and creamy. Pour into a bowl and refrigerate for at least 1 hour.

**4** Turn the lettuce onto a serving platter. Add the Caesar dressing and toss. Shell and quarter the hard-boiled eggs and add along with the chopped sun-dried tomatoes and parsley. Toss, then serve with the croûtons.

2 medium thick slices white bread or half a small baguette

3 tablespoons vegetable oil

2 small cos or little gem lettuces

3 eggs

6 sun-dried tomatoes in oil

2 tablespoons chopped fresh parsley

**FOR THE CAESAR DRESSING:**

1 egg

3 tablespoons lemon juice

salt and freshly milled pepper

6–8 drops Worcestershire sauce

1 clove garlic

25 g (1 oz) grated Parmesan cheese

100 ml (4 fl oz) olive oil

**Serves 4**
Preparation time: 25 minutes, plus chilling time
Cooking time: 7–8 minutes

# West Coast Fruit and Cheese Salad

2 x 227 g packets curd cheese

salt and freshly milled pepper

50 g (2 oz) broken walnuts

2 large oranges

½ small cantaloupe melon

225 g (8 oz) fresh cherries

1 x 50 g packet herb salad
  leaves

Fresh Herb Dressing (recipe
  below)

6–8 pecan nuts

2 tablespoons snipped fresh
  chives

**Serves 4**

Preparation time: 25 minutes,
  plus chilling time

**1** Turn the cheese into a bowl and, with a fork, work in a good seasoning of salt and freshly milled pepper. Coarsely chop the walnuts and put them on a sheet of greaseproof paper.

**2** Take heaped teaspoonfuls of the cheese mixture and roll them in the chopped walnuts until lightly coated. Transfer to a plate and chill until serving time.

**3** Take a slice from the top and base of each orange and cut away the peel and pith. Thinly slice the oranges. Remove the melon rind and seeds and cut the flesh into thin wedges. Rinse the cherries – I leave some of the stalks on because they look pretty.

**4** Toss the salad leaves in a little of the Fresh Herb Dressing and arrange in a shallow serving bowl. Add an arrangement of the fruits, nuggets of cheese and pecan nuts. Sprinkle with snipped chives and serve the remaining Fresh Herb Dressing separately.

**Fresh Herb Dressing:** Combine 3 tablespoons white wine vinegar, a seasoning of salt and freshly milled pepper, 1 teaspoon Dijon mustard, 2 teaspoons caster sugar and 175 ml (6 fl oz) olive oil. Mix well and stir in 3 tablespoons snipped fresh summer herbs – basil, chives, tarragon or parsley.

# Yellow Peppers with Tabbouleh

3 yellow sweet peppers

FOR THE TABBOULEH:

100 g (4 oz) bulgar wheat

6 ripe tomatoes

1 bunch (6–8) spring onions

½ cucumber

2 tablespoons chopped
  parsley

3 tablespoons chopped mint

juice 1 lemon

2 tablespoons olive oil

salt and freshly milled pepper

**Serves 6**

Preparation time: 20 minutes,
  plus soaking time

**1** Cut the sweet peppers in half from stalk to tip and scoop out the seeds. Place the peppers in a mixing bowl, pour over boiling water to cover and leave for 2–3 minutes to tenderise. Pour off the water and invert the peppers to drain. Set aside.

**2** Measure the bulgar into a medium mixing bowl. Stir in 150 ml (¼ pint) lukewarm water. Cover and leave for 15 minutes. Then fork the grains to loosen them. Scald the tomatoes in boiling water and peel away the skins. Halve and scoop out the seeds,then dice the tomato flesh. Trim the spring onions and chop all the white parts and some of the green stems. Cut the cucumber lengthways and across into small dice.

**3** Fork the tomato, spring onion and cucumber into the bulgar. Add the chopped parsley and mint, the juice of the lemon, olive oil and seasoning of salt and pepper. Toss to mix. Spoon the salad into the yellow pepper shells.

# Mint Pesto and Pasta Salad with Feta Cheese

*Delicate summery flavour – mint pesto is delicious, making the pasta green flecked.*

juice 1 lemon

4 tablespoons olive oil

1 tablespoon clear honey

salt and freshly milled pepper

4 tablespoons Mint Pesto
  (recipe below)

250 g (9 oz) penne (quills)

2 x 250 g packets feta cheese

250 g (9 oz) pitted green
  olives

**Serves 6**

Preparation time: 15 minutes

Cooking time: 8–10 minutes

**1** Start by making the Mint Pesto (see below). The recipe quantities make more than you will need for this dressing but it is delicious and will soon be used up. Combine the lemon juice, olive oil, honey and a seasoning of salt and freshly milled pepper in a large mixing bowl. Stir in the measured quantity of mint pesto.

**2** Add the pasta to a saucepan of boiling salted water, stir until the water reboils and boil for 8–10 minutes. Drain well, then add the hot pasta to the mint pesto dressing and toss. Allow to cool. Meanwhile break the feta cheese into bite-sized pieces. Add the feta cheese and green olives to the salad and toss. Turn onto a large platter and serve.

**Mint Pesto:** Strip the leaves from about 25 g (1 oz) fresh mint and drop them into a food processor bowl. Add 50 g (2 oz) toasted almonds, 1 teaspoon caster sugar, the grated rind of 1 lemon, 50–75 g (2–3 oz) grated Parmesan cheese and a seasoning of salt and freshly milled pepper. Cover and buzz to a coarse purée. Add 100 ml (4 fl oz) olive oil and buzz again for a few seconds to make the pesto – the texture should be gritty.

# Cold Stuffed Sweet Peppers

**1** Take a slice from the top of each pepper and reserve. Then scoop out and discard the seed box from inside each one and shake out any loose seeds. Set peppers aside while preparing the stuffing.

**2** Peel and finely chop the onion and peel and crush the garlic. Heat the oil in a saucepan. Add the onion and soften for a few minutes. Stir in the garlic and then the rice and fry a few moments more. Gradually stir in 300 ml (½ pint) boiling water. Add the tomato purée, a seasoning of salt and freshly milled pepper, the sugar and sultanas. Cover with the pan lid and cook gently for 15–20 minutes until the rice is softened and the liquid absorbed. Draw off the heat and fork in the chopped mint.

**3** Heat the oven to 180°C (350°F or gas no. 4). Pack spoonfuls of the stuffing into each pepper shell and replace the pepper lids. Place the filled peppers, close together, in a casserole dish. Add 4 tablespoons cold water, cover with the casserole lid (or kitchen foil). Set in the heated oven and bake for 40 minutes to 1 hour until the peppers are quite tender. Let the peppers cool slowly in the covered dish – they will wrinkle up attractively.

**4** Arrange the cold peppers on a serving platter, drizzle with extra olive oil and serve.

4 medium yellow or red sweet
  peppers
olive oil to serve

FOR THE RICE STUFFING:

1 medium onion
2–3 cloves garlic
3 tablespoons olive oil
100 g (4 oz) risotto rice
1 tablespoon concentrated
  tomato purée
salt and freshly milled pepper
1 teaspoon caster sugar
25 g (1 oz) sultanas
2 tablespoons chopped fresh
  mint

**Serves 4**
Preparation time: 30 minutes,
  plus cooling time
Cooking time: 1–1¼ hours


# Spinach and Avocado Salad with Hot Bacon Dressing

**1** Wash and thoroughly dry the spinach leaves and place in a salad bowl. Trim the spring onion, then chop all the white and some of the green stems. Peel, stone and cut the avocados into large cubes. Add the spring onions and avocado to the spinach.

**2** Cut the bread into small cubes, discarding the crusts. Trim and cut the bacon across into thin strips and place in a frying pan. Cook, stirring over a medium heat until the fat has begun to run and the bacon starts to brown. Add 1 tablespoon of the olive oil and the bread cubes and continue to cook until both bacon and bread cubes are crisp and brown. Remove both from the pan and keep warm.

**3** Peel and crush the garlic. Add the remaining olive oil to the frying pan, add the garlic and stir for a moment. Stir in the vinegar and bring to the boil. Season the dressing with salt and freshly milled pepper, pour over the spinach and toss to shine the leaves. Add the warm bacon and bread cubes, toss again and serve.

250 g (9 oz) fresh salad spinach
1 bunch (6–8) spring onions
2 ripe avocados
2 medium thick slices white
  bread
5–6 smoked back bacon
  rashers
3 tablespoons olive oil
1 clove garlic
1 tablespoon red wine vinegar
salt and freshly milled pepper

**Serves 3**
Preparation time: 20 minutes
Cooking time: 5–6 minutes

# Ravioli with Roasted Peppers and Olive Salad

**1** Heat the grill and set the grill rack at least 7.5 cm (3 inches) from the heat source. Halve, deseed and quarter the peppers. Arrange the peppers, skin side up, on a baking tray and brush with olive oil. Place under the preheated grill until the skins are charred and blistered. Turn the peppers over, brush with olive oil and return to the heat until the peppers are tender. Transfer to a plate and cool.
**2** Add the ravioli to boiling salted water with 1 tablespoon olive oil. Simmer 6 minutes or according to packet instructions, then drain.
**3** Turn the ravioli into a large mixing bowl. Add 2 tablespoons of the Honey Mustard Dressing and toss. Let the pasta cool but do not chill. Add the olives and remaining dressing and toss again. Turn the pasta onto a serving platter. Add the roasted peppers and serve.

**Honey Mustard Dressing:** Combine 2 tablespoons wholegrain mustard, 3 tablespoons white wine vinegar, 2 tablespoons clear honey, 100 ml (4 fl oz) olive oil and a good seasoning of salt and freshly milled pepper.

2 yellow sweet peppers
3–4 tablespoons olive oil
300 g (11 oz) ricotta and
 spinach-filled ravioli
50 g (2 oz) black olives
Honey Mustard Dressing
 (recipe below)

**Serves 3**
Preparation time: 15 minutes
Cooking time: 12 minutes

# Green Bean Salad with Chilli Dressing

**1** Top the beans but leave the tails, then cut beans in half. Add to a pan of boiling salted water, bring back to a simmer and cook for 3–4 minutes until barely tender, then drain. Plunge the beans into a bowl of cold water to cool.
**2** Trim the courgettes and pare the skin along the ridges, leaving a striped effect. Cut the courgettes in half. Slice pieces lengthways, then stack slices and cut lengthways again into thin strips.
**3** Halve and deseed the sweet pepper. Slice the pepper pieces lengthways and across into small dice. Combine all the vegetables in a bowl. Add the chopped parsley. Pour the Spicy Chilli Dressing over the bean salad and toss to mix.

**Spicy Chilli Dressing:** Combine 3 tablespoons white wine vinegar, 2 tablespoons sweet chilli sauce and 1 tablespoon soft brown sugar and stir. Add a seasoning of salt and pepper, 1 peeled and crushed clove of garlic, 100 ml (4 fl oz) olive oil and 1 teaspoon dried crushed chilli flakes. Stir or shake to mix.

450 g (1 lb) thin French beans
3 medium courgettes
1 yellow sweet pepper
3 tablespoons chopped fresh
 parsley
Spicy Chilli Dressing (recipe
 below)

**Serves 8**
Preparation time: 15 minutes
Cooking time: 3–4 minutes

# Raw Vegetable Salad with Honey Dressing

3 new carrots
2.5 cm (1 inch) fresh ginger
3 stalks celery
¼ cucumber
1 green sweet pepper
2 dessert apples
juice ½ lemon
100 g (4 oz) green grapes
100 g (4 oz) fresh dates
50 g (2 oz) walnut pieces
Honey Dressing (recipe
  below)
1 banana
wholemeal or walnut bread
  slices to serve

**Serves 4**

Preparation time: 25 minutes
Cooking time: 4–5 minutes

**1** Pare and grate the carrots. Pare the piece of ginger, then slice lengthways thinly. Stack the slices and cut again into matchstick thin slivers. Add the ginger to a pan of boiling water and boil for 2 minutes. Drain and pat dry. Put the carrot and ginger in a large mixing bowl.

**2** Trim, string and slice the celery stalks. Pare the cucumber, cut in half lengthways, scoop out the seeds. Slice lengthways and across into dice. Halve and deseed the green pepper then cut lengthways and across to finely chop. Add to the carrots.

**3** Quarter, core and slice the apples. Squeeze over the juice of ½ lemon and toss the slices to keep the colour. Wash the grapes and seed them, if necessary. Squeeze the fresh dates to pop them out of their skins. Slice lengthways, remove the stones and slice the dates again into slivers. Spread the walnut pieces on a baking tray and toast in a hot oven or under the grill for 2–3 minutes to bring up the flavour. Leave the walnuts to cool.

**4** Add the fruit (not the walnuts) to the salad ingredients and toss to mix. Add the Honey Dressing and toss again. Chill until serving time – not more than 2 hours.

**5** Just before serving, peel and slice in the banana and add the walnuts. Toss and turn into a large shallow serving bowl. Serve wholemeal or walnut bread slices to mop up the delicious juices.

**Honey Dressing:** Combine 2 tablespoons lemon juice, 2 tablespoons clear honey, 75 ml (3 fl oz) olive oil and a seasoning of salt and freshly milled pepper. Stir well to mix.

# Mixed Tomato Salad

**1** Using a small vegetable knife, cut out the stalk from the standard and plum tomatoes. Slice the standard tomatoes across, the plum lengthways and cherry in half. Peel and thinly slice the onions, separate out the rings.

**2** Layer the tomatoes and onions in a serving dish, contrasting the different tomatoes to get an attractive effect. Sprinkle the layers with sugar, salt and freshly milled pepper. Let the salad marinate for at least 2 hours.

**3** Before serving, spoon over the vinegar and olive oil, then sprinkle with parsley.

1.1 kg (2½ lb) ripe tomatoes – standard, plum and cherry in reasonable proportions
2 white salad onions
1 teaspoon caster sugar
salt and freshly milled pepper
1 tablespoon red wine vinegar
4 tablespoons olive oil
2 tablespoons coarsely snipped fresh flat leaf parsley

**Serves 8**
Preparation time: 15 minutes, plus marinating time

# Marinated Mini Vegetables

900 g (2 lb) mixed baby
  vegetables, rinsed and
  trimmed: mini corn, baby
  carrots, small courgettes,
  new potatoes or baby
  squash
3 tablespoons olive oil
1 tablespoon white wine
  vinegar
salt and freshly milled pepper
2 tablespoons chopped fresh
  parsley and chives

**Serves 8**
Preparation time: 10 minutes,
  plus marinating time
Cooking time: 15–20 minutes

**1** Select a colourful choice of vegetables. Cook all the vegetables in boiling salted water, or steam – mini corn and carrots will need about 7 minutes; courgettes, new potatoes and squash, up to 10 minutes. Whichever cooking method you choose, you want the vegetables to retain some bite.

**2** Drain and place the vegetables in a bowl. Add the olive oil, wine vinegar and a seasoning of salt and freshly milled pepper to the hot vegetables. Turn them and leave to marinate as they cool so that they absorb the flavours from the marinade. When cold, add the chopped parsley and chives and stir to mix.

# White Bean Salad with Gremolata

2 x 432 g tins cannellini beans
2 stalks celery
1 medium red onion
salt and freshly milled pepper
FOR THE GREMOLATA:
15 g (½ oz) fresh parsley
3 cloves garlic
1 lemon
75 ml (3 fl oz) olive oil
50 ml (2 fl oz) red wine
  vinegar

**Serves 6**
Preparation time: 20 minutes,
  plus marinating time
Cooking time: 5 minutes

**1** Turn the beans into a colander, rinse them under cold water, drain well and place them in a bowl. Trim the celery stalks, then slice lengthways and across to chop finely. Peel and finely chop the red onion. Add the celery and onion to the beans.

**2** Pick off the curly parsley tops (discard stalks) and place in a food processor. Add the peeled cloves of garlic and 2–3 long pieces of pared lemon rind (use a vegetable peeler). Squeeze the lemon juice and reserve. Add the olive oil and buzz to chop the mixture finely.

**3** Turn the parsley mixture into a saucepan. Add the vinegar and bring to a simmer. Pour the hot dressing over the bean salad. Add a seasoning of salt and milled pepper and the reserved lemon juice. Mix and leave to marinate for at least 1 hour before serving.

# Marinated Tomatoes with Chive Cream Dressing

**1** With a vegetable knife, cut out and discard the stalk of each tomato. Scald the tomatoes and peel away the skins. Slice the tomatoes thickly into a serving dish. Season with salt and freshly milled pepper and add the sugar.

**2** Peel and crush the garlic. Add the garlic to the sliced tomatoes along with the vinegar and olive oil. Leave the salad to marinate for 1–2 hours so that the dressing draws the juices from the tomatoes.

**3** Combine the mayonnaise, cream and chives and pour over the tomato slices. Stir to mix up the dressing. Serve chilled.

700 g (1½ lb) ripe tomatoes
salt and freshly milled pepper
1 teaspoon caster sugar
1–2 cloves garlic
1 tablespoon red wine vinegar
3 tablespoons olive oil
2 tablespoons mayonnaise
3 tablespoons double cream
2 tablespoons chopped fresh
 chives

**Serves 4–6**
Preparation time: 15 minutes,
 plus marinating time

# Marinated Coleslaw Salad

**1** Cut the cabbage half into two and slice away the core. Then, using a sharp kitchen knife, shred very finely across the wedges to make fine slivers and put them in a salad bowl. Trim the spring onions and chop all the white and some of the green stems. Add to the cabbage.

**2** Pare and grate the carrot. Trim the celery stalks, snap each one in half and pull away the strings, then cut celery lengthways and across into fine dice. Cut the apricots into fine slivers. Add the carrot, celery and apricots to the salad bowl.

**3** In a small mixing bowl, stir the sugar with 2 tablespoons boiling water until the sugar has dissolved. Stir in the vinegar, a good seasoning of salt and freshly milled pepper and the olive oil. Add to the salad and toss well. Leave in a cool place and allow to marinate for at least 2 hours before serving.

½ small white cabbage
1 bunch (6–8) spring onions
1 medium carrot
3 stalks celery
50 g (2 oz) ready-to-eat dried
 apricots
2 tablespoons caster sugar
2 tablespoons white wine
 vinegar
salt and freshly milled black
 pepper
2 tablespoons olive oil

**Serves 6**
Preparation time: 20 minutes,
 plus marinating time

# Thai Chicken Salad with Celery, Cucumber and Coriander

**1** Trim the chicken breasts. Place, skin side uppermost, on a roasting rack standing in a roasting tin. Brush the chicken skin with oil and season with salt and freshly milled pepper. Roast at 200°C (400°F or gas no. 6) for 30–35 minutes. Baste occasionally but do not turn the pieces.

**2** Cut the cucumber across into 5 cm (2 inch) lengths, halve and discard the seeds and slice into thin matchsticks. Trim the celery, cut the stalks the same size and cut lengthways into slivers. Trim the spring onions, cut off the green tops and finely chop the white stems. Enclose the salad vegetables in a polythene bag and chill until serving time. For the dressing, combine the peanut butter, lemon juice, soft brown sugar, soy sauce and vegetable oil. Whisk until the dressing is smooth, then add a seasoning of salt and pepper and the sesame oil.

**3** Toss the salad vegetables, toasted cashews and chopped coriander in the olive oil and a seasoning of salt and pepper. Spoon into a salad serving bowl. Remove the bone (skin, too, if you prefer) from the roast chicken pieces and cut the chicken into chunky pieces. Toss the chicken in the satay dressing and spoon over the salad greens. Toss before serving.

2–3 part-boned chicken
   breasts
olive oil for brushing
salt and freshly milled pepper
½ cucumber
2 stalks celery
1 bunch (6–8) spring onions
50 g (2 oz) toasted cashew
   nuts
2 tablespoons chopped fresh
   coriander
1 tablespoon olive oil

**FOR THE DRESSING:**
2 tablespoons smooth peanut
   butter
2 tablespoons lemon juice
1 tablespoon soft brown sugar
2 tablespoons dark soy sauce
75 ml (3 fl oz) vegetable oil
salt and freshly milled pepper
1 teaspoon sesame oil

**Serves 4**
Preparation time: 30 minutes,
   plus chilling time
Cooking time: 30–35 minutes

# Wild Rice Salad with Marinated Fruits

100 g (4 oz) wild rice

100 g (4 oz) long grain brown rice

600 ml (1 pint) vegetable stock

1 tablespoon grated fresh ginger

rind and juice 1 lemon

2 tablespoons clear honey

½ ripe galia melon

½ ripe pineapple

2 ripe avocados

3 tablespoons olive oil

1 tablespoon soy sauce

salt and freshly milled pepper

1 bunch (6–8) spring onions

½ small cucumber

fresh mint to garnish

**Serves 4**

Preparation time: 20 minutes, plus marinating time

Cooking time: 35–40 minutes

**1** Put the wild rice, brown rice and vegetable stock into a saucepan. Bring to the boil, stirring. Reduce the heat to a simmer, cover with the pan lid and cook the rice gently for 35–40 minutes until the grains are tender and the liquid is absorbed. Turn the rice into a mixing bowl.

**2** Into a second mixing bowl put the grated ginger, grated lemon rind and honey and stir to mix. Pare the melon and pineapple and dice into large chunky pieces. Add the fruits to the honey mixture and stir to mix. Leave to marinate for 45–60 minutes – the juices will run from the fruits forming the basis of a dressing.

**3** Peel and cut the avocados into chunky pieces. Reserve 1 tablespoon of the lemon juice for the dressing, then toss the avocado in the remaining juice. Spear alternate pieces of avocado, melon and pineapple on each of 8 satay sticks. To the fruit juices add the reserved lemon juice, olive oil, soy sauce and a seasoning of salt and freshly milled pepper.

**4** Trim the spring onions then finely slice the white and some of the green. Leave the cucumber unpeeled, then cut it first lengthways and then crossways into fine dice. Add the spring onions, cucumber and the prepared dressing to the rice and toss all the ingredients. Turn the mixture into a serving bowl. Pile the skewered fruits on top, then garnish with the mint and serve.

# Chicory, Carrot and Apple Salad

3 heads chicory

3 medium carrots

1 bunch (6–8) spring onions

2 tart green-skinned juicy dessert apples

1 teaspoon caster sugar

4–5 tablespoons Vinaigrette Dressing (recipe below)

2 tablespoons chopped fresh parsley

**Serves 4–6**

Preparation time: 15 minutes

**1** Trim any outer bruised leaves from the chicory, then take a slice from the base and with a knife point, scoop out the core from the stem ends. Cut the chicory into 1 cm (½ inch) slices across the leaves, separate out the shreds and put them in a salad bowl.

**2** Peel and coarsely grate the carrots. Trim the spring onions and chop all the white and some of the green stems. Peel, core and coarsely grate the apples. Add the carrots, spring onions and apples to the salad bowl, sprinkle over the sugar, and toss together. Add the Vinaigrette Dressing and the parsley and toss to mix.

**Vinaigrette Dressing:** Combine 2 tablespoons white wine vinegar, 1 teaspoon Dijon mustard, a seasoning of salt and pepper and 100 ml (4 fl oz) olive oil, and mix until well blended.

# Couscous and Chickpea Salad

**1** Start by preparing the dressing. Combine the grated lemon rind and juice, the vinegar, honey, salt and pepper and the olive oil. Mix well, making sure the honey has dissolved. Set aside.

**2** Measure 400 ml (¾ pint) water into a saucepan. Add the salt and 1 tablespoon of the olive oil. Bring to the boil, stir in the couscous and draw off the heat. Cover with the pan lid and leave undisturbed for at least 5 minutes. Then fork through the grains and turn the couscous into a mixing bowl. Add the dressing and cool to room temperature – the couscous will soak up the dressing.

**3** Heat the grill to hot and set the grill rack 7.5 cm (3 inches) from the heat source. Peel the onions leaving them whole. Cut each one into 4 thick slices and set them on a baking tray. Use the remaining 2 tablespoons olive oil to brush the onion slices. Set under the heat and grill until browned then separate into rings.

**4** Drain and rinse the chickpeas. Trim the spring onions, then chop all the white and some of the green stems. Cut the sun-dried tomatoes into pieces. Add the chickpeas, spring onions, sun-dried tomatoes and chopped mint and parsley to the couscous and toss. Turn the salad into a bowl and scatter with the grilled onion rings.

1 teaspoon salt
3 tablespoons olive oil
225 g (8 oz) couscous
2 medium onions
1 x 440 g tin chickpeas
1 bunch (6–8) spring onions
6–8 sun-dried tomatoes
2 tablespoons each chopped
  fresh mint and parsley

FOR THE DRESSING:
rind and juice 1 lemon
1 tablespoon wine vinegar
1 tablespoon clear honey
salt and freshly milled pepper
75 ml (3 fl oz) olive oil

**Serves 4–6**
Preparation time: 30 minutes
Cooking time: 5 minutes

# Cakes, Cookies and Bread

There is nothing so good as home baking, just the smell of it wafting through the house creates excitement. There's a huge variety of recipes in this chapter. Some can be blended in a food processor, others just stirred in the mixing bowl. Mouthwatering frostings, glazes and additions make them even more delicious.

*Raisin Bran Muffins, Apple Streusel Muffins, Raspberry Pecan Muffins and Glazed Lemon Muffins*

# Raisin Bran Muffins

225 g (8 oz) wholemeal flour

3 teaspoons baking powder

½ teaspoon salt

100 g (4 oz) soft brown sugar

100 g (4 oz) oatbran

100 g (4 oz) seedless raisins

150 ml (¼ pint) natural
  yoghurt

1 egg

75 ml (3 fl oz) sunflower oil

**Makes 12**

Preparation time: 10 minutes

Baking time: 15–20 minutes

**1** Heat the oven to 200°C (400°F or gas no. 6). Oil a 12-cup muffin or deep bun tray (tartlet size will not do).

**2** Combine the flour, baking powder, salt and sugar (rubbed through a sieve if it is lumpy), oatbran and raisins in a large mixing bowl. Stir well to distribute the baking powder.

**3** Make the yoghurt up to 300 ml (½ pint) with water. Combine the yoghurt liquid with the egg and oil. Mix to break up the egg. Add the yoghurt mixture to the dry ingredients and mix only until the flour is evenly moistened. Do not overmix – it should be lumpy.

**4** Spoon the batter into the prepared tray, filling each section about half full. Put the tray of muffins in the preheated oven and bake for 15–20 minutes. Let the baked muffins stand in the tray for about 5 minutes, then loosen the sides, turn over the tray and knock them out with a sharp tap. Serve the muffins warm.

**Apple Streusel Muffins:** Mix 50 g (2 oz) soft brown sugar, 50 g (2 oz) chopped pecan nuts and ½ teaspoon ground cinnamon and set aside. Sift 275 g (10 oz) plain flour, 3 teaspoons baking powder and ½ teaspoon salt into a second bowl. Add 75 g (3 oz) caster sugar and mix. Combine 1 egg, 300 ml (½ pint) milk and 75 ml (3 fl oz) oil. Core, peel, then grate 1 tart apple and add to the liquid ingredients, then add this to the flour. Mix until the flour is moistened. Sprinkle the pecan mixture on the unbaked muffins. Bake as above.

**Raspberry Pecan Muffins:** Sift 225 g (8 oz) plain flour, 3 teaspoons baking powder and ½ teaspoon salt into a mixing bowl. Add 100 g (4 oz) caster sugar and 50 g (2 oz) chopped pecan nuts and mix. Combine 1 egg, 300 ml (½ pint) milk and 75 ml (3 fl oz) oil. Mix to break up the egg. Add the milk mixture and 100 g (4 oz) fresh rasp- berries to the dry ingredients; mix until flour is moistened. Bake as above.

**Glazed Lemon Muffins:** Sift 275 g (10 oz) plain flour, 3 teaspoons baking powder and ½ teaspoon salt into a mixing bowl. Add 75 g (3 oz) caster sugar, finely grated rind 1 lemon and mix. Combine 1 egg with 300 ml (½ pint) milk and 75 ml (3 fl oz) oil. Mix to break up the egg. Add the milk mixture to the dry ingredients and mix until the flour is moistened. Bake as above. Warm the juice of 1 lemon with 50 g (2 oz) caster sugar and 50 g (2 oz) butter. Then dip the hot baked muffins in the warm glaze.

# Spiced Honey Cake

**1** Heat the oven to 160°C (325°F or gas no. 3). Butter a baking (or roasting) tin of approximately 30 x 22.5 cm (12 x 9 inches) and line with a strip of greaseproof paper cut the width of the tin and long enough to overlap opposite ends.

**2** Sift the flour, bicarbonate of soda, salt, cinnamon, ginger and cloves into a large mixing bowl and make a well in the centre. Measure the butter, sugar and honey into a saucepan and warm over a low heat until the ingredients are runny, but not hot. Crack the eggs into a measuring jug and make up to 300 ml (½ pint) with milk (or natural yoghurt). Mix with a fork to break up the eggs.

**3** Pour the melted ingredients into the sifted flour mixture. Add the eggs and milk. Using a wooden spoon, stir to blend the ingredients then beat to a smooth batter. Pour into the prepared cake tin and spread level. Sprinkle with the flaked almonds. Set in the heated oven and bake for 50 minutes to 1 hour. Cool in the tin – tastes best after a day or so. Keeps well.

450 g (1 lb) self-raising flour
½ teaspoon bicarbonate of soda
1 teaspoon salt
1 teaspoon ground cinnamon
½ teaspoon ground ginger
½ teaspoon ground cloves
175 g (6 oz) butter
250 g (9 oz) caster sugar
450 g (1 lb) clear honey
3 eggs
milk – see recipe
25 g (1 oz) flaked almonds

**Cuts into 24 pieces**
Preparation time: 20 minutes
Baking time: 50 minutes–1 hour

# Apricot and Banana Bread

**1** Heat the oven to 180°C (350°F or gas no. 4). Grease a 22.5 x 12.5 x 7.5 cm (9 x 5 x 3 inch) loaf pan and line with a strip of greaseproof paper cut the width of the base and long enough to overlap both ends. Sift the flour and salt into a large mixing bowl.

**2** Add the butter cut into pieces and rub in with fingertips. Stir in the sugar. Snip the dried apricots into pieces. Set aside 6 pecan nuts and coarsely chop the remainder. Add the apricots, chopped pecan nuts and sultanas and mix. Peel and mash the bananas and add along with the eggs – no extra liquid is required. Beat with a wooden spoon to blend the ingredients.

**3** Spoon the mixture into the prepared tin and spread level. Arrange the reserved pecan nuts on top. Place in the preheated oven and bake for 1–1¼ hours. Allow to cool in the tin for 20 minutes, then loosen the unlined sides and lift the banana bread out by the paper ends. Leave until completely cold. Serve sliced and buttered.

225 g (8 oz) self-raising flour
½ teaspoon salt
100 g (4 oz) butter
175 g (6 oz) caster sugar
100 g (4 oz) ready-to-eat dried apricots
50 g (2 oz) pecan nuts
100 g (4 oz) sultanas
450 g (1 lb) ripe bananas (weight with skins on)
2 eggs

**Makes 1 large loaf**
Preparation time: 20 minutes
Baking time: 1–1¼ hours

# Carrot and Pineapple Cake

225 ml (8 fl oz) sunflower oil

275 g (10 oz) soft brown
  sugar

1 teaspoon vanilla essence

4 eggs

150 g (5 oz) plain flour

150 g (5 oz) wholemeal flour

2 teaspoons bicarbonate of
  soda

2 teaspoons ground cinnamon

225 g (8 oz) carrots, peeled
  and grated

1 x 432 g tin unsweetened
  crushed pineapple, with juice
  reserved

100 g (4 oz) sultanas

**FOR THE GLAZE:**

175 g (6 oz) icing sugar

1–2 tablespoons pineapple
  juice

flaked almonds for sprinkling


**Makes 12 pieces**

Preparation time: 25 minutes

Baking time: 45 minutes–1 hour

**1** Heat the oven to 180°C (350°F or gas no. 4). Grease a 22.5 x 32.5 cm (9 x 13 inch) shallow baking pan or small roasting tin.

**2** Put the oil, brown sugar, vanilla essence and eggs into a large mixing bowl. Break up the eggs with a fork. Sift in both flours, the bicarbonate of soda and cinnamon. Tip in any bran still in the sieve. Stir with a wooden spoon, then beat to a smooth batter. Mix in the grated carrot, crushed pineapple and sultanas. Pour into the prepared tin and level out. Bake for 45 minutes to 1 hour. Cool in the pan.

**3** Combine the sifted icing sugar with sufficient pineapple juice to make a smooth coating. Spoon over the surface of the carrot and pineapple cake in streaky lines. Sprinkle with the flaked almonds. When set, cut into squares and lift from the tin to serve.

---

## Katie's Tip

The American Chiffon Cake opposite is inverted after baking
so it cools without compacting and retains a light texture.
Rest opposite edges of the baking pan on tins (fruit or
vegetables) of similar height.

# Chiffon Cake with Baked-On Butterscotch Topping

**1** Heat the oven to 160°C (325°F or gas no. 3). Select a 20 x 3.5 cm (8 x 1½ inch) square baking pan and leave ungreased. Separate the eggs, cracking the yolks into a large mixing bowl and the whites into a second smaller bowl. Add the oil, 75 ml (3 fl oz) water and vanilla essence to the egg yolks and stir to blend.

**2** Place a sieve over the bowl and into it sift the flour, baking powder and 100 g (4 oz) of the caster sugar. Using a wooden spoon, stir to blend, then beat to a smooth cake batter. Whisk the egg whites until stiff, sprinkle in the remaining sugar, half at a time, and beat until glossy. Fold into the batter using the cutting edge of a tablespoon. Pour the mixture into the baking pan and bake for 30–35 minutes. Cool by inverting the pan (see Katie's Tip opposite).

**3** Melt the butter for the topping in a saucepan. Add the sugar, nuts and cream. Stir over a low heat to blend and bring to a simmer. Spoon hot topping onto cake and spread over the surface. Place the cake in a baking pan under the grill until the frosting bubbles. When cold, loosen sides, give pan a sharp tap and the cake should drop out.

3 eggs
50 ml (2 fl oz) vegetable oil
½ teaspoon vanilla essence
150 g (5 oz) plain flour
1 teaspoon baking powder
175 g (6 oz) caster sugar

**FOR THE BUTTERSCOTCH TOPPING:**

50 g (2 oz) butter
100 g (4 oz) soft brown sugar
50 g (2 oz) chopped walnuts
1 tablespoon double cream

**Makes 9 pieces**
Preparation time: 30 minutes
Baking time: 30–35 minutes

# Orange Chocolate Chip Cake

**1** Heat the oven to 160°C (325°F or gas no. 3). Grease and base line a 20 x 5 cm (8 x 2 inch) sponge cake tin, then dust with flour. Finely chop the chocolate and the walnut pieces with a kitchen knife and set aside.

**2** Sift the flour and baking powder into a large mixing bowl. Add the margarine, sugar, eggs, orange rind and juice. Using a wooden spoon stir first to blend the ingredients, then beat well for 1 minute to get a smooth cake batter. Fold in the chocolate and walnut pieces. Spoon the mixture into the prepared cake tin and spread level. Set in the heated oven and bake for 35–40 minutes. Let cool in the baking tin 5 minutes then turn onto a rack. Leave until cold.

**3** Sift the icing sugar for the glaze into a mixing bowl. Measure the cocoa powder, caster sugar and butter into a saucepan and add 2 tablespoons cold water. Stir over a moderate heat until the sugar has dissolved, then bring to the boil. Stir the hot chocolate syrup into the sifted icing sugar to make a thick coating consistency. Pour over the cake and spread evenly, leave until cold when the glaze will set.

75 g (3 oz) plain chocolate
75 g (3 oz) walnut pieces
200 g (7 oz) self-raising flour
2 teaspoons baking powder
175 g (6 oz) soft margarine
175 g (6 oz) caster sugar
3 eggs
1 tablespoon grated orange rind
2–3 tablespoons orange juice

**FOR THE CHOCOLATE GLAZE:**

75 g (3 oz) icing sugar
1 tablespoon cocoa powder
25 g (1 oz) caster sugar
15 g (½ oz) butter

**Cuts into 8–10 slices**
Preparation time: 20 minutes
Baking time: 35–40 minutes

# Chocolate Mousse Cake

90 g (3½ oz) plain flour, plus
  extra for dusting
15 g (½ oz) cocoa powder
4 eggs
100 g (4 oz) caster sugar
40 g (1½ oz) butter
FOR THE MOUSSE FILLING:
200 g (7 oz) plain chocolate
1 x 142 ml carton soured
  cream
2 tablespoons dark rum
300 ml (½ pint) double cream
FOR THE FROSTING:
150 g (5 oz) plain chocolate
1 x 142 ml carton soured
  cream
chocolate flakes
cocoa powder for dusting

**Cuts into 8–10 slices**
Preparation time: 40 minutes,
  plus cooling and chilling time
Baking time: 25–30 minutes

**1** Heat the oven to 180°C (350°F or gas no. 4). Grease a 22.5 x 5 cm (9 x 2 inch) sponge cake tin or 22.5 cm (9 inch) spring-clip pan and base-line with a circle of greaseproof paper. Dust the tin with flour, turn over and tap to knock out any excess flour. Sift the recipe flour and cocoa powder onto a square of greaseproof paper.
**2** Crack the eggs into a mixing bowl and add the caster sugar. Put the butter in a small bowl and set in a warm place to melt. Set the mixing bowl over a saucepan a quarter filled with hot (not boiling) water and whisk the egg and sugar mixture until thick and light – about 10 minutes. Remove the bowl from the heat and whisk for a moment more.
**3** Sift the flour mixture over the surface of the beaten egg mixture and fold in gently. When the flour has almost disappeared add the melted butter and mix everything together. Pour into the prepared cake tin and spread level. Set in the preheated oven and bake for 25–30 minutes. Let the baked sponge cool in the tin for 5 minutes, then turn out and leave until cold.
**4** Slice the sponge cake in half. Break the chocolate for the mousse filling into a small bowl, set over a saucepan of hot (not boiling) water until melted. Remove from the heat, add the soured cream and rum and stir until smooth. In a larger bowl whip the cream to a soft custard consistency. Add the chocolate mixture and gently mix together – it will be quite thick. Turn the mixture onto the base half of the sponge cake and spread evenly, then cover with the top half of the sponge cake. Chill for at least 4 hours or overnight until filling is firm.
**5** Break the chocolate for the frosting into a medium mixing bowl and melt (see above). Add the soured cream and mix to a smooth shiny frosting. Turn the frosting onto the chilled sponge cake, spread over the top and around the sides. Sprinkle with the chocolate flakes. Chill until serving time, then dust over with some cocoa powder.

# Coffee Yule Log

**1** Heat the oven to 220°C (425°F or gas no. 7). Grease an oblong 32.5 x 22.5 cm (13 x 9 inch) biscuit tin (with edges) and line with a strip of greased, greaseproof paper long enough to cover the base and overlap opposite ends. Sift the flour and cornflour twice and add the ground almonds.

**2** Crack the eggs and egg yolk into a mixing bowl and add the sugar. Set over a saucepan a quarter filled with hot (not boiling) water and beat until the mixture leaves a trail as it drops from the whisk. Remove the bowl from the heat and continue whisking for a few minutes more until the mixture is quite thick.

**3** Sift the flour mixture evenly over the surface and fold in gently using a tablespoon. Turn into the prepared tin and spread level. Set in the preheated oven and bake for 6–8 minutes. Let the baked roulade cool for 1 minute. Loosen the sides and turn it out onto a clean tea cloth. Cover with a second cloth and leave until cold.

**4** For the buttercream, cream the butter until soft in a mixing bowl. Measure the granulated sugar and 100 ml (4 fl oz) water into a saucepan. Stir over a low heat until the sugar has dissolved – check there are no sugar grains round the insides of the pan. Bring the syrup to the boil and cook for 1½ minutes. Meanwhile whisk the egg yolks until creamy – an electric mixer helps with this last stage of the recipe. With the beater going, pour the hot syrup into the eggs in a slow steady stream. The mixture will come up thick and light. Continue to beat for about 5 minutes or until the mixture feels cool to the touch. Beat in the soft butter a tablespoon at a time until the buttercream is light and fluffy. Stir in the coffee essence.

**5** Strip the baking paper from the cooled roulade and trim the sides with a kitchen knife. Turn so that the baked surface faces upwards and transfer it to a sheet of greaseproof paper. Spread half the coffee buttercream over the roulade and roll up from the short end. Spread the remainder over the outer surface and with the prongs of a fork, mark the surface attractively. Rinse the glacé fruits in warm water to remove the sugar coating, then cut into chunky pieces and use them for decoration. Chill for several hours or overnight. Slice the cake straight from the refrigerator using a kitchen knife dipped in hot water for clean cuts.

40 g (1½ oz) plain flour
1 tablespoon cornflour
15 g (½ oz) ground almonds
2 eggs
1 egg yolk
75 g (3 oz) caster sugar

**FOR THE COFFEE BUTTERCREAM:**

250 g (9 oz) unsalted butter
250 g (9 oz) granulated sugar
3 egg yolks
2 tablespoons coffee essence
green glacé cherries, angelica, candied pineapple and orange slices to decorate

## Cuts into 8 slices

Preparation time: 1 hour, plus cooling and chilling time
Baking time: 6–8 minutes

# Chocolate Pecan Crumb Cake

225 g (8 oz) self-raising flour

1 teaspoon baking powder

115 g (4½ oz) butter

100 g (4 oz) caster sugar

50 g (2 oz) plain chocolate

1 egg

150 ml (¼ pint) milk

FOR THE CRUMB TOPPING:

50 g (2 oz) self-raising flour

1 teaspoon ground cinnamon

75 g (3 oz) soft brown sugar

50 g (2 oz) butter

50 g (2 oz) chopped pecan
  nuts

**Cuts into 12 slices**

Preparation time: 25 minutes

Baking time: 30–40 minutes

**1** Heat the oven to 180°C (350°F or gas no. 4). Butter a 20 cm (8 inch) square or 27.5 x 17.5 cm (11 x 7 inch) oblong baking pan – and line with a strip of greaseproof paper cut the width of the base and long enough to overlap opposite ends.

**2** Prepare the crumb topping. Rub the flour, cinnamon and soft brown sugar through a sieve into a small bowl. Add the butter in pieces and rub in with fingertips. Add the chopped pecans, mix and set aside.

**3** Sift the flour and baking powder into a mixing bowl. Add 100 g (4 oz) of the butter in pieces and rub in with fingertips. Add the sugar and mix. Break the plain chocolate into a small bowl, add the remaining 15 g (½ oz) of butter and put somewhere warm to melt.

**4** Combine the egg and milk and mix with a fork to break up the egg. Add to the dry ingredients and mix to a soft batter. Turn the mixture into the prepared tin and spread level. Spoon the melted chocolate mixture over the batter. Then, with a knife, cut through the batter several times for a marbled effect. Level the mixture again if necessary. Sprinkle with the pecan crumb topping and press gently.

**5** Set in the preheated oven and bake for 30–40 minutes. Turn out, remove the paper and cut into 12 pieces to serve warm.

# American Doughnuts

450 g (1 lb) self-raising flour
½ teaspoon ground cinnamon
1 tablespoon baking powder
75 g (3 oz) caster sugar
2 eggs
225 ml (8 fl oz) milk
50 g (2 oz) melted butter
sunflower oil for frying
icing sugar for dusting

**Makes 12–14 ring
doughnuts and holes**

Preparation time: 20 minutes,
   plus chilling time
Cooking time: 15 minutes

**1** Sift the flour, cinnamon and baking powder into a large mixing bowl. Add the sugar and stir. Combine the eggs, milk and melted butter and mix well to break up the eggs. Add the egg mixture to the dry ingredients and mix to a soft dough. Cover and chill the mixture for 1 hour – to firm up.

**2** Turn the dough onto a floured work surface and roll to a depth of not less than 1 cm (½ inch). Using a floured 7.5 cm (3 inch) round cutter, stamp out doughnut circles, then using a smaller 2.5 cm (1 inch) cutter remove holes from the centres to make ring doughnuts. Reserve the holes. Reroll the dough trimmings to make the last few doughnuts.

**3** Heat the oil for frying – no more than 3.5 cm (1½ inches) in depth in a large 25 cm (10 inch) frying pan. Slide 2–3 doughnuts at a time into the hot oil with a wide spatula. Turn the doughnuts as they rise to the surface and fry for 2–3 minutes until golden brown on both sides. Drain on kitchen paper and, while still hot, shake the doughnuts in a polythene bag of sifted icing sugar to dust them. Repeat with all the doughnut rings and holes.

# Coffee Brownies

**1** Heat the oven to 160°C (325°F or gas no. 3). Butter a 27.5 x 17.5 cm (11 x 7 inch) rectangular baking tin. Measure the instant coffee granules into a medium-sized mixing bowl. Add 1 tablespoon of boiling water and stir to dissolve the granules. Add the chocolate chips and the butter. Set the bowl over a pan, quarter-filled with hot (not boiling) water and stir until the chocolate and butter have melted. Remove from the heat.

**2** Stir the sugar into the melted ingredients, then beat in the eggs one at a time. Set a sieve over the mixing bowl, measure in the flour and sift into the chocolate mixture. Beat the mixture until smooth and shiny. Stir in the walnuts. Pour the batter into the prepared cake tin and spread level. Set in the preheated oven and bake for 35 minutes. Cool in the baking tin.

**3** To make the icing, combine the instant coffee granules with 1 tablespoon boiling water in a small bowl. Stir in sufficient icing sugar to make a runny icing. Drizzle over the baked brownies. When the icing has set, cut the brownies into squares.

1 tablespoon instant coffee granules

1 x 115 g packet plain chocolate chips

100 g (4 oz) butter

175 g (6 oz) soft brown sugar

2 eggs

75 g (3 oz) self-raising flour

75 g (3 oz) broken walnuts

FOR THE ICING:

½ teaspoon instant coffee granules

50–75 g (2–3 oz) sifted icing sugar

**Makes 12**

Preparation time: 20 minutes

Baking time: 35 minutes

# Fork Butter Cookies

*Crunchy cookies that are good with or without the coffee buttercream filling.*

**1** Sift the flour and ginger onto a plate. In a mixing bowl cream the butter and sugar until soft and light, add half the flour and mix until smooth, then add the remaining flour and knead to a dough. Or, measure the butter and sugar into a food processor bowl and mix until soft and creamy. Add the flour and ginger and process to a rough dough. Turn the dough into a mixing bowl and draw together with fingertips.

**2** Heat the oven to 190°C (375°F or gas no. 5). Take walnut-sized pieces of the dough and roll into balls. Set on ungreased baking trays and flatten each cookie with a wet fork. Set in the heated oven and bake for 10–12 minutes or until lightly coloured. Cool for 2 minutes on the baking trays, then transfer to a wire cooling rack.

**3** In a mixing bowl cream the butter, icing sugar and coffee essence for the buttercream filling. Spread the filling over half the baked cookies and sandwich with the remainder.

350 g (12 oz) plain flour

1 teaspoon ground ginger

225 g (8 oz) butter

175 g (6 oz) caster sugar

FOR THE FILLING:

50 g (2 oz) butter

100 g (4 oz) sifted icing sugar

1 teaspoon coffee essence

**Makes 24**

Preparation time: 20 minutes, plus cooling time

Baking time: 10–12 minutes

# Chocolate Chip Bars

50 g (2 oz) skinned hazelnuts
100 g (4 oz) butter
50 g (2 oz) soft brown sugar
75 g (3 oz) caster sugar
1 egg
1 teaspoon vanilla essence
150 g (5 oz) self-raising flour
1 x 115 g packet plain
   chocolate chips

**Makes 30**
Preparation time: 15 minutes
Baking time: 11–13 minutes

**1** Heat the oven to 190°C (375°F or gas no. 5). Lightly grease a 32.5 x 22.5 cm (13 x 9 inch) baking tin with shallow sides. Put the hazelnuts on a baking tray and set in the oven as it is heating up to toast them. Once they are toasted, buzz in a food processor to chop coarsely, then set aside.

**2** Measure the butter, brown sugar and caster sugar into a food processor bowl and buzz to cream. Add the egg and vanilla essence and buzz to mix. Add the flour and chopped hazelnuts and process to a soft dough. Turn the mixture into the prepared tin and spread level, paying special attention to the corners. Sprinkle the chocolate chips evenly over the dough.

**3** Set in the preheated oven for 1 minute to allow the chocolate chips to melt, then run a knife blade through the dough to 'marble' the mixture. Return to the oven and bake for a further 10–12 minutes or until firm to the touch and light brown. Cool in the tin, then cut lengthways and across into bars.

# Christmas Shortbread

150 g (5 oz) plain flour
50 g (2 oz) semolina or
   ground almonds
50 g (2 oz) caster or soft
   brown sugar
100 g (4 oz) chilled butter
whole unblanched almonds,
   plain chocolate chips,
   chopped, mixed-colour glacé
   cherries or crushed sugar
   lumps to decorate

**Makes 8 pieces**
Preparation time: 10 minutes
Baking time: 35–40 minutes

**1** Measure the plain flour, semolina or ground almonds and sugar into a food processor bowl. Cover and blend using the on/off switch to mix. Add the chilled butter in medium dice. Cover and blend to coarse crumbs (do not let mixture form a dough). Or cream the butter and sugar in a mixing bowl until soft, then stir in the dry ingredients until the mixture forms coarse crumbs.

**2** Heat the oven to 160°C (325°F or gas no. 3). Lightly butter a 20 cm (8 inch) fluted flan tin. Turn in the mixture and press down firmly, then prick all over with a fork. Add the desired decoration (see below) and press in gently. Bake 35–40 minutes. Remove from the heat and cool until warm, then cut into triangles. Cool in the baking tin and break into pieces when cold. Transfer to a lidded storage tin.

**Variations are as follows:** With whole almonds placed around the rim, add the ground almonds and caster sugar to the mixture; with a scattering of chocolate chips or chopped glacé cherries, use semolina and caster sugar; with crushed sugar lumps, use semolina and brown sugar.

# Southern Corn Bread

**1** Heat the oven to 200°C (400°F or gas no. 6). Oil a 22.5 x 12.5 x 7.5 cm (9 x 5 x 3 inch) large loaf pan and line it with a strip of greaseproof paper that is cut to fit the width of the base and long enough to overlap the opposite ends. Sift the flour, baking powder and salt into a medium mixing bowl. Add the cornmeal and the caster sugar and mix.

**2** In a smaller bowl combine the egg, milk and melted butter. Mix with a fork to break up the egg. Add the liquid to the dry ingredients and stir until the ingredients are blended. Turn the batter into the prepared tin and spread level. Set in the preheated oven and bake for 30 minutes.

**3** Let the corn bread cool in the tin for 2 minutes, then loosen the sides and turn the bread onto a rack. Cut it in slices and serve warm. Corn bread is also delicious when it is toasted.

150 g (5 oz) plain flour
3 teaspoons baking powder
½ teaspoon salt
150 g (5 oz) cornmeal
50 g (2 oz) caster sugar
1 egg
300 ml (½ pint) milk
25 g (1 oz) butter, melted

**Makes 1 large loaf**
Preparation time: 15 minutes
Baking time: 30 minutes

# Poppy Seed Breadsticks

*These breadsticks are packed close in the baking tin, which means that they come out of the oven with soft sides and crisp tops.*

**1** Heat the oven to 190°C (375°F or gas no. 5). Sift the flour, baking powder and salt into a large mixing bowl. Add the butter, cut into pieces, and rub in with fingertips. Combine the eggs and milk and mix with a fork to break up the eggs.

**2** Melt the butter in a medium-sized roasting tin, or deep-sided baking tin, 20 x 25 cm (8 x 10 inches). Pour the egg and milk mixture into the dry ingredients all at once and, using a table knife, mix to a soft dough in the bowl. Turn the dough onto a floured work surface, knead once or twice, then roll the dough to an oblong, just a little smaller than your choice of tin. With a floured kitchen knife cut the dough in half lengthways and then across in 2.5 cm (1 inch) wide slices.

**3** Working from the top left, turn each breadstick in the melted butter, coating all sides, and push it to the top left of the baking tin. Repeat with each breadstick, arranging them close together in two rows - you will have to squeeze in the last one if you've been doing it right. Sprinkle the breadsticks with poppy seeds. Set in the preheated oven and bake for 15 minutes or until well risen. Turn onto a wire rack and separate the breadsticks – they will come apart quite easily.

450 g (1 lb) self-raising flour
2 teaspoons baking powder
½ teaspoon salt
100 g (4 oz) butter
2 eggs
150 ml (¼ pint) milk
50 g (2 oz) butter for the tin
poppy seeds to decorate

**Makes 16**
Preparation time: 20 minutes
Baking time: 15 minutes

# Dark Chocolate Chunk and Hazelnut Cookies

300 g (11 oz) self-raising flour

225 g (8 oz) plain chocolate

100 g (4 oz) skinned toasted hazelnuts

225 g (8 oz) butter

175 g (6 oz) caster sugar

100 g (4 oz) soft brown sugar

2 eggs

1 teaspoon vanilla essence

**Makes 48**

Preparation time: 20 minutes

Baking time: 10–12 minutes

**1** Heat the oven to 190°C (375°F or gas no. 5). Sift the flour onto a plate (or sheet of greaseproof paper) and set aside. With a kitchen knife, cut the chocolate into chunky pieces. If the hazelnuts you buy are not toasted, pop them into a baking tin and set in the oven as it is heating up to brown them. Chop the nuts coarsely.

**2** In a large mixing bowl, cream the butter and both sugars until soft and light. Mix the eggs and vanilla essence with a fork. Beat the egg into the creamed mixture gradually in about 3 parts, mixing each addition well before adding the next. Add half the flour and mix through the dough. Then add the remaining flour and mix in, before adding the chocolate pieces and hazelnuts.

**3** Drop heaped teaspoonfuls onto ungreased baking trays – not more than 6 to a tray as they will spread during cooking. Set in the preheated oven and bake for 10–12 minutes or until they are just golden. Let them cool on the tray for a couple of minutes before transferring to a wire cooling rack.

**White Chocolate Chunk and Brazil Nut Cookies:** Follow the basic recipe above using 250 g (9 oz) self-raising flour and 50 g (2 oz) cocoa powder sifted together to make a chocolate batter. Add chunks of white chocolate instead of plain, and chopped Brazil nuts in place of hazelnuts.

---

### Katie's Tip

If you're short on baking trays for cookie-making, get a production line going using several sheets of foil or baking parchment, cut to the size of your baking tray. As each batch of cookies comes out of the oven, lift it off, paper and all, and simply slide a fresh sheet with unbaked cookies into place.

# Chocolate Meringues

*These little biscuits can be served on their own or with other chocolaty desserts.*

**1** Heat the oven to 150°C (300°F or gas no. 2). Line 2 baking trays with baking parchment. Put the egg whites in a large mixing bowl. Place the sifted icing sugar, the cocoa powder and 25 g (1 oz) of the caster sugar in a separate bowl and mix.

**2** Beat the egg whites to stiff peaks, then whisk in the remaining 50 g (2 oz) caster sugar, one tablespoon at a time. Beat well after each addition to make a glossy meringue.

**3** Add the sugar and cocoa mixture: using a tablespoon, gently and evenly fold into the meringue to make a chocolate mixture. Take 2 dessertspoons and drop the chocolate meringue mixture in mounds onto the lined trays. Alternatively, spoon the mixture into a large piping bag fitted with a rosette nozzle and pipe the mixture in fingers. Sprinkle the meringues with roasted hazelnuts.

**4** Set the meringues in the preheated oven and immediately lower the temperature to 110°C (225°F or gas no. ¼). Leave in the warm oven for 2 hours. Turn off the oven heat and leave the meringues for a further 1 hour. Drizzle with melted chocolate to decorate.

2 egg whites
25 g (1 oz) icing sugar
1 tablespoon cocoa powder
75 g (3 oz) caster sugar
1 tablespoon roasted chopped
 hazelnuts
50 g (2 oz) melted chocolate
 to drizzle

**Makes 12**

Preparation time: 20 minutes
Baking time: 2 hours, plus
 drying-off time

Tif Hunter

# Date and Walnut Loaf Cake

*Moist and easy to slice with discernable chunks of dates and walnuts – keep for 24 hours before serving.*

1 x 225 g block pressed dates
1 large lemon
1 teaspoon bicarbonate of
   soda
100 g (4 oz) butter
100 g (4 oz) soft brown sugar
1 egg
225 g (8 oz) self-raising flour
100 g (4 oz) broken walnuts

**Makes 1 loaf cake**
Preparation time: 25 minutes,
   plus cooling time
Baking time: 1–1¼ hours

**1** Grease and base-line a 22.5 x 12.5 x 7.5 cm (9 x 5 x 3 inch) oblong tin. Roughly chop the dates and place in a medium bowl. Finely grate the lemon rind and add to the dates. Squeeze the lemon juice into a measuring jug. Sprinkle the bicarbonate of soda over the chopped dates. Make up the lemon juice to 225 ml (8 fl oz) with boiling water and add to the bowl. Stir well and leave until cold.

**2** Heat the oven to 160°C (325°F or gas no. 3). Beat the butter and sugar until smooth and creamy. Lightly mix the egg and stir into the creamed mixture. Stir in the date mixture. Sift the flour into the mixture. Stir until well mixed. Reserve about 25 g (1 oz) of the broken walnuts and stir the remainder into the cake mixture.

**3** Spoon the mixture into the prepared tin and spread level. Sprinkle with the reserved walnuts. Set in the preheated oven and bake for 1–1¼ hours. Cool in the baking tin for 15 minutes, then turn onto a wire rack. Slice to serve.

# Boiled Fruit Cake

*A boiled fruit cake is very old-fashioned and always moist textured, the addition of crushed pineapple makes this variation particularly flavoursome. The decoration is optional, you can easily serve the cake plain.*

**1** Lightly grease and line a 20 cm (8 inch) round cake tin. Measure the mixed fruit, butter, sugar, mixed spice and bicarbonate of soda into a large saucepan. Stir in the crushed pineapple. Bring to the boil over a medium heat, stirring constantly. Boil for 3 minutes. Remove from the heat and leave the mixture to cool in the saucepan.

**2** Heat the oven to 160°C (325°F or gas no. 3). Put a sieve over the saucepan, measure in the flour and salt and sift into the cold fruit mixture. Mix the eggs with a fork to break them up and add to the pan. Stir all the ingredients to mix them thoroughly.

**3** Spoon the mixture into the prepared cake tin and spread level. Set in the preheated oven for 1¾–2 hours. Let the cake cool in the baking tin before turning out.

**4** To decorate, brush the cake top with just a little sieved apricot jam, then place on 3 well-drained rings of pineapple. Blend the icing sugar with sufficient lemon juice to make a thick glacé icing, then drizzle over the pineapple pieces and cake top.

450 g (1 lb) mixed dried fruit
175 g (6 oz) butter
175 g (6 oz) granulated sugar
1 teaspoon mixed spice
1 teaspoon bicarbonate of soda
1 x 432 g tin crushed pineapple
350 g (12 oz) self-raising flour
pinch of salt
3 eggs

FOR DECORATION:

1 tablespoon sieved apricot jam
3 rings tinned pineapple
75 g (3 oz) sifted icing sugar
squeeze of lemon juice

**Makes 1 x 20 cm (8 inch) cake**
Preparation time: 20–30 minutes,
   plus cooling time
Baking time: 1¾–2 hours

---

### HIGHLY DECORATED

**Scrolls:** Thinly spread melted chocolate on a marble slab and let it cool, then shave off scrolls with a kitchen knife. Aim to catch the chocolate as it's beginning to set. Any left over can be scraped up and remelted.

**Cuts:** Scrape the edge of a chocolate bar with a swivel vegetable peeler – a chocolate bar at room temperature is easier to work with than one too chilled. Dark and white chocolate cuts look good mixed together.

**Drizzle:** Spoon melted plain chocolate into a small greaseproof paper piping bag (set in a mug to hold it steady). Fold to close and snip the point. Drizzle chocolate over cakes or cookies.

# Desserts

Desserts are a fitting finale to any meal. They are always delicious, hot or cold, fruity or chocolaty. Fruits have wonderful colours and shapes and delicious juicy flavours. Chocolate, vanilla and yoghurt are just some of the other irresistible flavours which make an appearance in this chapter.

*Chocolate Choux with Sweetened Mascarpone and Berries*

# Chocolate Choux with Sweetened Mascarpone and Berries

50 g (2 oz) plain flour

15 g (½ oz) cocoa powder

50 g (2 oz) butter

1 teaspoon caster sugar

2 eggs

beaten egg to glaze

FOR THE SWEETENED
MASCARPONE:

1 x 250 g tub mascarpone

2 tablespoons sifted icing
  sugar

2 tablespoons soured cream

350 g (12 oz) mixed
  raspberries and blueberries

icing sugar for dusting

Chocolate Sauce to serve
  (recipe below)

**Serves 8**

Preparation time: 40 minutes,
  plus cooling time

Cooking time: 25 minutes

**1** Heat the oven to 220°C (425°F or gas no. 7). Lightly grease two baking trays. Sift the flour and cocoa powder onto a square of greaseproof paper.

**2** Measure 150 ml (¼ pint) cold water into a saucepan. Add the butter and sugar. Set over a moderate heat and allow the butter to melt, then bring to a full rolling boil. Tip in all the flour at once and stir over the heat until the mixture forms a thick paste that comes away from the sides of the pan – about 1 minute. Draw the pan off the heat.

**3** Allow the paste to cool until the hand can be comfortably held against the sides of the pan. Lightly mix the eggs. Beat the eggs into the paste a little at a time – it's easiest to do this in a food processor. When ready the mixture should be smooth and glossy – like thick cream.

**4** Place 4 tablespoons of the mixture, well apart, on each tray. Brush each one with a little egg glaze over the tops. Set in the preheated oven and bake for 25 minutes until well risen and firm. Cut a slash in the sides of each choux bun to let the steam escape and give them another few minutes' baking time – so they will stay firm without collapsing. Allow to cool and store airtight – a tightly closed polythene bag is fine.

**5** For the filling, combine the mascarpone, sifted icing sugar and soured cream to make a soft creamy filling. Pick over the fruits. Slice each chocolate choux in half, spoon on sweetened mascarpone and soft fruits then cover with the choux top. Arrange on a serving platter and dust generously with icing sugar. Serve with warm Chocolate Sauce.

**Chocolate Sauce:** Measure 50 g (2 oz) caster sugar, 4 tablespoons water and 15 g (½ oz) butter into a saucepan and stir over a low heat to form a syrup. Bring to the boil and draw off the heat. Add 100 g (4 oz) plain chocolate broken in pieces – it will melt in the hot mixture. Stir with a whisk until the sauce is smooth. Add ½ teaspoon vanilla essence. Pour the sauce into a warmed jug for serving.

# Strawberry Soufflé

**1** Tie a band of double-thickness greaseproof paper tightly with string around the outside of a 15–17.5 cm (6–7 inch) soufflé dish to form a collar, standing at least 5 cm (2 inches) above the rim of the dish. Set the dish on a large plate so it's easy to move around.

**2** Hull the strawberries and buzz to a purée in a blender or food processor, or press through a sieve. Put 4 tablespoons of cold water into a teacup, sprinkle in the gelatine and soak for 5 minutes.

**3** Pour half of the strawberry purée into a pan, add 175 g (6 oz) of the sugar and the soaked gelatine. Stir over a low heat to dissolve the sugar and gelatine, but do not let it boil. Take off the heat and pour into a large mixing bowl. Add the rest of the strawberry purée and the lemon juice and leave until the mixture cools, then begins to thicken and show signs of setting.

**4** Whip the cream to the consistency of soft custard. Whisk the egg whites until they are stiff, add the rest of the sugar and beat again until glossy. Add the cream to the strawberry mixture and, when half folded through, add the beaten egg whites. Mix the ingredients gently but thoroughly.

**5** Pour into the prepared soufflé dish. The mixture should rise above the rim of the dish to be held in place by the paper collar. Chill for at least 4 hours, until the soufflé has set.

**6** Loosen the string and gently peel the paper away from the soufflé. Serve with pouring cream or extra sliced and sugared strawberries – or both.

900 g (2 lb) fresh strawberries
2 tablespoons powdered
  gelatine
225 g (8 oz) caster sugar
juice 2 lemons
300 ml (½ pint) double cream
3 egg whites

## Katie's Tip

To get the maximum light, airy texture in a cold soufflé (or mousse) combine the ingredients when they are all of a similar consistency: whipped cream, beaten egg whites and gelatine base on the point of setting. Stir the gelatine mixture occasionally as it cools and look out for a change in the texture. Always add cream first, then egg whites.

**Serves 8**
Preparation time: 30 minutes,
  plus chilling time
Cooking time: 2–3 minutes

# Raspberry Clafoutis

**1** Sift the flour into a mixing bowl and make a well in the centre. Crack in the eggs and add half the milk. Stir with a wooden spoon from the centre, gradually drawing in the flour from around the sides of the bowl to make a thick batter. Stir in the rest of the milk and the vanilla essence. Chill until serving time.

**2** Heat the oven to 200°C (400°F or gas no. 6). Put the butter into a roasting or baking tin of approximately 30 x 20 cm (12 x 8 inches). Set in the preheated oven until the butter is melted and bubbling – more than 2–3 minutes. Pour in the batter, then sprinkle the raspberries all over the batter. Return to the oven and bake for 30–40 minutes.

**3** Sprinkle the hot clafoutis with caster sugar. Then cut in portions and serve warm with spoonfuls of thick yoghurt or cream.

100 g (4 oz) plain flour
2 eggs
175 ml (6 fl oz) milk
1 teaspoon vanilla essence
40 g (1½ oz) butter
250 g (9 oz) raspberries
caster sugar for dusting

**Serves 4–6**
Preparation time: 10 minutes, plus chilling time
Cooking time: 30–40 minutes

# Peach Crumb Pie

**1** Sift the flour into a mixing bowl. Add the butter cut into pieces and rub in with fingertips. Set 100 g (4 oz) of the mixture aside for the crumb topping. To the remainder add 2 tablespoons cold water and mix to a pastry dough.

**2** Roll the pastry to a circle and use to line a 22.5 cm (9 inch) pie plate. Trim the pastry edges. To the reserved crumb mixture add the soft brown sugar and cinnamon, then rub the mixture with your fingertips or mix with a fork until the crumbs gather in small clumps.

**3** Heat the oven to 190°C (375°F or gas no. 5). Cut into the peaches following the natural line around the fruit from the stalk end. Then twist the halves in opposite directions to separate and remove the centre stone. Skin and slice the peaches.

**4** Combine the cornflour and caster sugar and mix well. Add to the peach slices, tossing until evenly coated. Spoon the peaches into the pastry shell, spreading the slices to distribute them evenly and mound a little in the centre.

**5** Sprinkle over the crumb topping to cover. Set in the preheated oven and bake for 40 minutes. Delicious hot or cold.

225 g (8 oz) plain flour
150 g (5 oz) butter
50 g (2 oz) soft brown sugar
½ teaspoon ground cinnamon
8–9 ripe peaches
1 tablespoon cornflour
25 g (1 oz) caster sugar

**Serves 6**
Preparation time: 30 minutes
Cooking time: 40 minutes

# Lemon Ice Cream Cake

100 g (4 oz) almond
  macaroons
1 x 397 g tin full cream
  sweetened condensed milk
finely grated rind and juice of
  4 lemons
300 ml (½ pint) double cream
700 g (1½ lb) raspberries to
  serve

**Serves 8**

Preparation time: 40 minutes,
  plus chilling and freezing time

**1** Select a loaf pan or oblong freezer container that will hold about 900 ml (1½ pints). Line with foil cut to the width of the base and long enough to overlap at opposite ends. Chill while preparing the ice cream.

**2** Put almond macaroons in a larger freezer bag, crush to fine crumbs with a rolling pin.

**3** Turn condensed milk into a mixing bowl. Add the lemon rind and juice. Stir well, the mixture will thicken. Whip the cream to a soft custard consistency. Add to the lemon mixture, folding in well.

**4** To assemble the cake, spoon a quarter of the lemon mixture into the chilled container and spread level. Sprinkle over a quarter of the macaroon crumbs to make a layer. Freeze for 10 minutes. Repeat the layering and freezing process until the ice cream crumbs are used up, ending with a layer of crumbs. Cover with a strip of foil and freeze for at least 4 hours or overnight.

**5** Unmould the frozen cake onto a serving plate and, using the foil ends, draw it out of the container. Peel away the foil and place the cake in the refrigerator for 30 minutes. Slice with a kitchen knife and serve with fresh raspberries.

# Chocolate and Crème Fraîche Mousse

150 g (5 oz) plain chocolate
15 g (½ oz) unsalted butter
3 eggs
1 x 200 g tub crème fraîche

**Serves 8**

Preparation time: 20 minutes,
  plus chilling time

**1** Break the chocolate into a mixing bowl and add the butter. Set over a saucepan of hot water (off the heat) and stir occasionally until the chocolate has melted. Remove the bowl from the heat.

**2** Separate the eggs, cracking the whites into a second bowl and stirring the yolks into the melted chocolate one at a time. Add the crème fraîche and stir until the mixture is smooth and creamy.

**3** Whisk the egg whites to stiff peaks and fold into the chocolate mixture. Pour into 8 individual ramekin dishes (or a single bowl) and chill for at least 4 hours or overnight until the mixture is firm. Shaved chocolate on sliced strawberries makes a pretty decoration if you want to add something.

# Chocolate Marquise

**1** In a saucepan dissolve the sugar in 3 tablespoons cold water and bring to the boil. Draw off the heat, add the rum and allow to cool.
**2** Break the chocolate into a small bowl, set over a saucepan of hot (not boiling) water and stir until melted. Cream the butter and sifted icing sugar until soft. Then beat in the egg yolks one at a time. Finally, stir in the melted chocolate.
**3** Divide the sponge fingers into 3 lots of 6 sponge fingers. Dip the first lot (one or two at a time) into the warm rum syrup and allow to soak for a moment. Arrange a neat row of 6 on a serving dish and spread with a layer of chocolate cream.
**4** Cover with the second layer of dipped sponge finger and another layer of chocolate cream. Top with the final layer of soaked sponge fingers and sprinkle over any unused syrup. Finally spread the rest of the chocolate cream over and around the sides.
**5** Decorate with grated chocolate or sprinkle with chopped walnuts and chill for several hours or overnight. Slice for serving.

50 g (2 oz) granulated sugar
2 tablespoons rum
100 g (4 oz) plain chocolate
100 g (4 oz) butter
100 g (4 oz) sifted icing sugar
4 egg yolks
1 packet (18) sponge finger
  biscuits
grated chocolate or chopped
  walnuts to decorate

**Serves 6**
Preparation time: 50 minutes,
  plus chilling time
Cooking time: 10 minutes

# Glazed Strawberry Shortcake

175 g (6 oz) plain flour
100 g (4 oz) butter
50 g (2 oz) icing sugar
1 egg yolk
700 g (1½ lb) fresh
  strawberries
1 tablespoon strawberry
  conserve
2 tablespoons redcurrant jelly
juice ½ lemon

**Serves 6–8**

Preparation time: 30 minutes,
  plus chilling time
Cooking time: 25 minutes

**1** Measure the flour into a food processor bowl, add the butter (chilled) in pieces and buzz to crumbs. Add the icing sugar and buzz to mix. Add the egg yolk and process until the dough clings in large lumps. Turn onto a floured surface and use your fingertips to draw the dough together into a smooth ball.

**2** On a floured surface roll the pastry to a 22.5 cm (9 inch) circle. Slide the pastry onto a baking tray, prick all over with a fork and press around the edge to decorate. Chill for 30 minutes.

**3** Heat the oven to 190°C (375°F or gas no. 5). Set the shortcake in the oven and bake for 20 minutes, or until golden and crisp and lightly browned around the edges. Allow to cool on the baking tray for 10 minutes, then slide onto a cooling rack and leave until cold.

**4** Hull the strawberries and pick them over. Place the shortcake on a flat serving plate and spread with strawberry conserve. Arrange the whole strawberries to cover the tart, place their tips upwards, within about 2.5 cm (1 inch) of the shortcake border.

**5** Place the redcurrant jelly and lemon juice in a pan and bring to a simmer – a gentle whisk will help the jelly to dissolve. Spoon the hot glaze over the berries. Serve cold cut into wedges, with thick cream.

# Hot Blackberry Trifle

**1** Spoon the blackberries into the base of a buttered 1.1 litre (2 pint) baking dish. Split the trifle sponge cakes and place cut side down over the fruit in an even layer and press gently.

**2** In a mixing bowl combine the whole eggs, egg yolks and caster sugar. Add the milk, cream and vanilla essence and whisk to mix. Strain the custard into a jug. Pour over the sponge cake and leave to soak for 15 minutes.

**3** Heat the oven to 180°C (350°F or gas no. 4). Place the baking dish in a larger roasting tin and pour around boiling water to the depth of about 2.5 cm (1 inch). Set in the preheated oven and bake for 40 minutes or until the custard has set.

**4** Whisk the egg whites to stiff peaks. Whisk in the sugar (one tablespoon at a time) and beat to a glossy meringue. Swirl the meringue over the top of the pudding. Sprinkle with the toasted flaked almonds. Return the pudding to the oven for long enough to brown the meringue – about 4–5 minutes. Serve warm.

225–275 g (8–10 oz) cultivated blackberries
6 trifle sponge cakes
3 eggs
3 egg yolks
25 g (1 oz) caster sugar
300 ml (½ pint) milk
300 ml (½ pint) single cream
1 teaspoon vanilla essence
**FOR THE MERINGUE:**
3 egg whites
175 g (6 oz) caster sugar
toasted flaked almonds

**Serves 6**
Preparation time: 25 minutes, plus soaking time
Cooking time: 45 minutes

# Swedish Apple Cake

**1** Buy a slab of ready-made Madeira cake – you'll find something suitable on any supermarket shelf. Break the cake into pieces and place in a food processor bowl. Cover and buzz to crumbs. Add the ground cinnamon and the finely grated lemon rind and buzz again. Turn the crumbs into a bowl.

**2** Peel, core and cut up the apples. Place in a saucepan with the squeezed juice of the lemon and 2 tablespoons cold water. Set over a moderate heat, cover with the pan lid and cook gently until the apples are quite soft – about 10 minutes. Stir to a purée. Add the sugar and sultanas and mix – the sugar will dissolve in the heat of the pan. Let the apple mixture cool.

**3** Heat the oven to 180°C (350°F or gas no. 4). Lightly butter a 20 cm (8 inch) cake tin with a loose bottom. Place one third of the cake crumbs over the base. Spoon over half the apple purée. Top with a second third of the cake crumbs, then the rest of the apple purée. Finally cover with the remaining crumbs.

**4** Set the cake in the preheated oven and bake for 20–25 minutes or until golden. Cool 10 minutes in the pan, then push the cake up – using the loose bottom – and lift out. Dust the cake with icing sugar. Serve warm or cold – nice with cream.

275 g (10 oz) butter Madeira cake – see method
½ teaspoon ground cinnamon
grated rind and juice 1 lemon
900 g (2 lb) cooking apples
50 g (2 oz) caster sugar
25 g (1 oz) sultanas
icing sugar for dusting

**Serves 6**
Preparation time: 20 minutes, plus cooling time
Cooking time: 20 minutes

# Extremely Thin Apple Slice

250 g (9 oz) puff pastry
40 g (1½ oz) butter
40 g (1½ oz) caster sugar
1 egg
50 g (2 oz) ground almonds
6 tart dessert apples
2 tablespoons apricot jam
1 tablespoon lemon juice

**Serves 6**

Preparation time: 15 minutes,
  plus chilling time
Cooking time: 20 minutes

**1** On a lightly floured surface, roll the pastry to an oblong the size of your baking tray – approximately 25 x 35 cm (10 x 14 inches). Slide the pastry onto the tray and chill for at least 30 minutes. Meanwhile, cream the butter and sugar until soft. Beat in the egg and almonds to make a smooth cream.

**2** Trim the edges of the pastry with a sharp knife to make a neat shape. Prick the centre area with a fork (to stop it from rising) and spread the almond cream over the pastry, leaving a 2.5 cm (1 inch) border all round.

**3** Heat the oven to 200°C (400°F or gas no. 6). Peel and core the apples, then cut in half. Slice each half, holding the slices in order. Press gently to flatten and fan out each piece. Set in three neat rows down the pastry – 4 sliced halves should fill one row.

**4** Set the tart in the preheated oven and bake for 20 minutes or until the pastry is risen and crisp and the apples tender. Meanwhile, warm the apricot jam and lemon juice and bring to a simmer. Spoon the hot glaze over the apple slices. Serve sliced lengthways into strips and across into portions.

# Baked Bananas with Orange Slices and Rum

25 g (1 oz) butter
6 firm ripe bananas
3 oranges
50 g (2 oz) soft brown sugar
2 tablespoons dark rum

**Serves 4**

Preparation time: 15 minutes
Cooking time: 20 minutes

**1** Heat the oven to 190°C (375°F or gas no. 5). Grease a baking dish with a little of the butter. Peel the bananas and arrange them together in the dish. Finely grate the rind of 1 orange over the bananas, then squeeze the juice and add it too. Take the remaining oranges and cut away the peel with a vegetable knife (round and round like an apple). Slice the oranges and tuck them in alongside the bananas.

**2** Sprinkle with the soft brown sugar and add the rest of the butter in flakes. Set in the preheated oven and bake for 20 minutes – by the time the bananas are ready, they will be soft and glazed. Add the rum about 5 minutes before the cooking time is up. Serve each hot banana with a few orange slices and the syrup from the baking dish spooned over.

# Italian Baked Peaches

**1** Crush the macaroons into coarse crumbs – in a polythene bag with a rolling pin is the easiest way. In a mixing bowl, cream the butter (at room temperature) and the sugar. Stir in the egg yolk. Add the crushed macaroons.

**2** Cut into the peaches following the natural line around the fruit from the stalk end (no need to skin them), then twist halves in opposite directions to separate. Remove each stone and scoop out a little of the peach pulp to make a deeper space for the filling.

**3** Add the peach pulp to the macaroon mixture and mix everything together. Take walnut-sized pieces of the mixture and press into each peach half.

**4** Heat the oven to 180°C (350°F or gas no. 4). Arrange the stuffed peaches in a single layer in a buttered baking dish. Set the dish in the preheated oven and bake for about 25 minutes. While the peaches are still hot from the oven, spoon over the port to make delicious juices, then serve.

100 g (4 oz) almond
  macaroons
25 g (1 oz) butter
50 g (2 oz) caster sugar
1 egg yolk
6 ripe peaches
2–3 tablespoons port

**Serves 6**
Preparation time: 20 minutes
Cooking time: 25 minutes

# Raspberry and Apple Open Tart

**1** Sift the flour into a mixing bowl. Add the butter in pieces and rub in with fingertips. Sprinkle over 2 tablespoons cold water and stir to moisten the mixture. Then with floured fingers, draw the ingredients together to form a dough. Turn the dough onto a floured work surface and knead for a moment. Chill dough until baking time.

**2** Heat the oven to 200°C (400°F or gas no. 6). Peel, core and slice the apples into a mixing bowl. Add the raspberries. Combine the caster sugar and cornflour, then sprinkle over the fruits and toss together to mix.

**3** Roll the pastry to a circle large enough to line a 22.5 cm (9 inch) pie plate with 5 cm (2 inches) to spare all round. Trim the pastry if uneven. Transfer the pastry to the pie plate allowing the excess to overhang the edge. Pile the fruits in the centre and spread evenly. Fold the overhanging edge inwards around the rim – the centre of the tart should remain uncovered.

**4** Set the tart in the preheated oven and bake for 30–35 minutes. Serve hot.

175 g (6 oz) plain flour
75 g (3 oz) butter
3 tart dessert apples
250 g (9 oz) raspberries
2 tablespoons caster sugar
1 tablespoon cornflour

**Serves 4–6**
Preparation time: 20 minutes,
  plus chilling time
Cooking time: 30–35 minutes

# Index